HOW TO BE A GOOD DAD

Stephen A. Bly

MOODY PRESS

CHICAGO

All Scripture quotations in this book are from the *New American Standard Bible,* © 1960, 1962, 1963, 1968, 1971, 1972, 1973, 1975, and 1977 by The Lockman Foundation, and are used by permission.

Library of Congress Cataloging-in-Publication Data

Bly, Stephen A., 1944-
　How to be a good dad.

　1. Fathers—United States. 2. Father and child—
United States. 3. Family—Religious life. I. Title.
HQ756.B58　　1986　　　　306.8'742　　　　86-2483
ISBN 0-8024-3571-8 (pbk.)

2 3 4 5 6 7 Printing/LC/Year 91 90 89 88 87 86

Printed in the United States of America

For Schmo and his sister, Squash

Contents

CHAPTER   PAGE

1. Staking Out the Claim   9
2. Caring Dads Wear Cowboy Hats   19
3. Caring Dads Build Phone Book Holders   27
4. Caring Dads Sing Solos   37
5. Caring Dads Treat the Family Like the Preacher's There   49
6. Caring Dads Keep the Office Door Open   59
7. Caring Dads Let Them Go   69
8. Caring Dads Are Zoo Keepers   79
9. Caring Dads Volunteer for the Christmas Play   89
10. Caring Dads Make Them Pull Weeds   97
11. Caring Dads Marry Them Off   107
12. Caring Dads Cry When They Leave Home   113
13. Caring Dads Leave the Door Open, the Porch Light On   123
14. Caring Dads Hug Moms   131

1

Staking Out the Claim

Joseph Walker.

Jedediah Smith.

Most history books stick them in the same paragraph. Some call them early Western explorers. Some call them trappers. Others might label them Indian fighters. Their Eastern contemporaries called them reckless and foolish. They preferred the simple name *mountain men.*

They both belonged to that uncontrollable band of restless men who crossed the Mississippi towards the unexplored wilderness between 1810 and 1840. To parallel what they did in our day, you would have to put together a spaceship in your backyard and set out to explore outer space on your own.

Both came West to the wilderness in their early twenties. They demonstrated toughness and leadership ability. Jedediah Smith was quickly recognized for his coolness and bravery. Bold, outspoken in his faith, he was grim, high-minded, and inflexible. His 668 beaver pelts displayed during the 1824-1825 season rank as an all-time record for any mountain man.

Looking for more beaver streams, Smith and fifteen companions headed out of the 1826 Cache Valley Rendezvous on a journey that would lead them to the Mexican land called Alta California. Smith made two such historic treks. On each one he promoted the typical mountain man way of doing things—push on, follow your hunches, blunder your way through, hang tough, drive to the end. From the Great Salt Lake, through bleak northern Arizona, and across the Mojave Desert, Smith directed his party of men. After three years and thirty-three men (twenty-six died along the way and two deserted), he had nothing to show for his efforts, not even a decent trail to California.

On the other hand, Joe Walker, who stood six feet at 200 pounds, hawk-beaked and bearded, blazed new trails in the wilds. A few years later, Walker rounded up a gang of trappers at the Green River Rendezvous and rode west to find a trail to California. Even tempered, able to command without offending, he delighted in exploring unknown regions. When the word spread that Joe Walker commanded a crew to California, long lines of trappers volunteered. He chose forty of the best.

His explorers began the trip with four horses apiece, sixty pounds of jerky per man, and all the gear needed for such a trip. He consulted local Indians along the way to chart his course across northern Nevada, along what's now called the Humbolt River, and finally to the Sierras. The first mountain crossing tried the hardiest of them, but after a rest on the large ranchos of California, they discovered a low altitude crossing (Walker Pass) to return home.

With foresight, common sense, and a good plan, Walker, unlike Smith before him, opened up the golden lands of California. His path marked the very foundation of the famous California Trail that beckoned miners and settlers by the thousands. His pass proved the most accessible. His men served as wagon masters of countless trips. Their stories of the warm fertile California climate charmed folks for the next 150 years.

Basic skills didn't separate Smith from Walker. Both were exceptional mountain men. Desire didn't make the difference. Both wanted to carve through those mountains. Walker reached his goal because he had a plan. He took the time to prepare in a proper manner.

That's why Joseph Walker succeeded, and Jedediah Smith failed.

There are a lot of differences between dads, too. But we've got a lot in common as well. We work hard. We enjoy our families. We care about our kids. We want to provide a world that's safe, peaceful, and beautiful for them. We hope they'll grow to be thoughtful, caring, intelligent, independent, successful children.

We care.

We really do care.

So why does it seem that some dads achieve much more than others? Some wind up with families that hum. Others find themselves bogged down with hassles and frustrations. What makes the difference?

Many times it's the same thing that separated Joe Walker from Jed Smith. One blunders along, hoping all will work out. The other plans, listens, prepares, and carries out a specific action intended to accomplish a goal. There's no such thing as an absolute guarantee in this life, of course. But the odds favor the Joe Walkers.

That's where this book can be of some help. I won't try to convince you to care about your family. I won't need to.

Here's what I offer to do. I'll help you discover a Bible principle or two, give you some ideas on how to put them into practice, share some sad and humorous incidents, and let you decide from there what you'll do.

The Old West lured many with its unlimited opportunities. It provided hardship and danger. A vast, new, wild world needed to be populated. A man could choose to run cattle, turn over the sod and farm, or dig for gold. Whichever the case, he needed to mark off the four corner posts of the property he claimed and file the proper papers at the nearest territorial courthouse. Those corner posts, or piles of rocks, delineated the boundaries of his domain. Within that boundary, he built his estate.

Building a winning family is similar. Sometimes little gets done because we've never taken time to set the boundaries. We wander aimlessly through unmarked prairies.

What are the corner posts of a winning family? Here are four suggestions.

First, I assume we all want to build quality into our family life. This deserves more than just surface agreement. Subtle and selfish wills can divert the best of intentions.

Gary attends every family conference in the county. He's the first to talk about the sad decline in family life in America. In fact, it's almost a slogan with him. Gary's running for a position in the state legislature. His campaign speeches are peppered with "Strengthen Family Life" themes.

Cathy, his wife, is a former beauty pageant queen. She conducts an early morning aerobics class on the local TV channel. Their two children attend a prestigious private school. Brad's a good tennis player who's been offered several scholarships this year. Tricia, their daughter, sings like a pro. But for now, the whole family's dedicated to one thing: getting Dad elected. As long as every member fulfills his part in this process, they're an ideal family.

But what if one of the members decides on another goal? Gary is content as long as he controls their direction. He sees his family as a necessary prop in achieving his own personal dreams.

That doesn't mean Gary doesn't love his family. He does. He's just never thought through whether he's building quality into his family life. He's too busy politicking. The truth is, any dad can fall into such a trap from time to time. We can claim great concern for our family, but the minute one of them behaves in a way that doesn't promote our pet image or ambition, we come unglued.

Second, I assume we're willing to work at building a winning family. Wanting a winner of a family involves a proper attitude. Willingness to work requires self-discipline. It means pushing the old bod when you'd rather just sit there in front of the TV. It means not merely planning an activity but carrying it out.

Randy, Tom, Bob, and Jerry have played golf every Saturday morning for almost ten years, ever since they starred on the local college team. But Bob dropped out last September. It was a tough choice for him. He'd just lowered his handicap to three. What a time to quit. But two considerations forced his decision.

He wanted to spend more uninterrupted time with his daughters, Carrie, age eight, and Amy, age six. Also, he wanted to give his wife, Nanci, some private time to herself.

It all came about when Carrie and Amy wanted to enroll in a gymnastics class that convened in a town twenty-three miles from home. The class met on Saturday mornings. Bob could have insisted that Nanci take the girls, but that meant one more morning of hassle for her. Instead, Bob said good-bye to the foursome at Riverside Golf Course and greeted the mornings at the Sunnyside Gym. Two happy daughters giggled through lunch at a fast food chain, while Nanci relished a whole morning to herself.

It took more than good intentions for Bob to carry it off. The polished persimmon woods idle away in the red leather golf bag. The club championship tourney yields one less entrant. It's spring. The fairway trees are in full bloom. The warm winds smell of new-mown greens, and nerves twitch with the excitement of the crack of a hit.

To invest in building a winning family cost Bob something.

Third, I assume that we're willing to recognize an authority higher than ourselves. One of the corner posts of a strong family is the Bible. As a practical guide for family matters, the Bible has proven its reliability. For thousands of years its wisdom has instructed the faithful. Today it remains the world's best-selling book. Even families who never attend church or claim direct knowledge of God base many of their actions on biblical principles. Those principles have sometimes been handed down from generation to generation until folks don't know where they originated. All they know is that they work.

Jeff's Uncle Ted took him aside on his wedding day. "Jeff," he advised, "never let the sun go down on your anger. If you and your wife argue, keep talking until you've solved it."

Jeff followed that advice. In fact, he'll tell you that's been one of the strengths of his twenty-three year-marriage. What Jeff didn't know, until just last year, was that Uncle Ted quoted the Bible (Ephesians 4:26).

Biblical principles work. They work year after year, century after century, because people don't change. Cultures change. Technology changes. Knowledge changes. But human nature is constant. For instance, the sibling rivalry of Cain and Abel (those first sons of Adam and Eve) repeats itself in millions and billions of families throughout earth's history.

Good reasons impel us to trust the Bible. Second Timothy 3:16

states: "All Scripture is inspired by God and profitable for teaching, for reproof, for correction, for training in righteousness." The greatest people in history acted on biblical principles and urged others to do the same. We've yet to discover any man better at dealing with people than Jesus. He not only validated the entire Old Testament with His life, but He left us, through inspired writers, twenty-seven new books to search.

Perhaps the best reason to try biblical principles is because they work. I'm a rather pragmatic guy. I suppose that comes from thirty years of living and working on a farm. At every equipment show I've attended, new product salesmen astound me with their claims. The products range from chemical hardpan solvents to mechanical asparagus planters. Anything can look good displayed in a brochure or parked in a cement floored exhibition hall. But I want to see it in action on the field. Show me how it dissolves *my* hardpan or plants *my* asparagus; then I'll tell you what I think of it.

I've been field-testing biblical principles for years. A family using biblical principles is a winning family. You can find testimonials all around you. Trust God's Word, and you'll have one firmly driven stake in the boundaries of quality family living.

Fourth, you've got to have a basic commitment to Jesus Christ. This marker's the simplest and the toughest at the same time. You've got to work at it. You've got to base your family life on biblical principles. But in addition, you need a personal friendship with God through His Son.

If you've already established that relationship—great! You know what I'm talking about, and you're ready to proceed. On the other hand, you may have never even considered it. You may be determined to stay as far away as possible from anything sounding religious. Or you may know all about the subject but have never made a firm pledge.

Each dad needs to make his own decision to believe that Jesus is exactly who He claims to be—to trust that He has done, is doing, and will do all that He states in the Bible.

Some men object to making such a personal commitment and feel that religious beliefs fall outside of public scrutiny. They may think of religion as anti-intellectual or as something that requires dependence rather than self-sufficiency. It may seem unmasculine. I should know—I used to have all those feelings myself.

Five years after marriage I liked what was happening. I had a loving, supportive wife and two bright, healthy, handsome sons. We lived in a comfortable house in the country. I spent my days on the farm, working the land as had my father and grandfather before me. I had everything the way I wanted it. I was no neurotic.

Yet there was still something missing. In quiet moments, when I dared to be honest with myself, I wondered, *Is this all there is to life?* Was it merely to be a seventy-year cycle of planting and harvesting, of eating and sleeping, of weekdays and weekends, of getting and spending, of growing older and older?

I had no zealous friends urging me on, not even a nagging wife, and only a casual connection to church. I lived the good life, according to this world's standards, but I wanted something more. I wanted a first-class quality life, a winning life. And that seemed out of my grasp. So in a fit of introspection I suggested to my wife that we should read the Bible together because "It's been lots of good help to other people. Maybe it will benefit us."

We searched through discarded books in the garage to find one and soon developed a nightly pattern of reading after we tucked the kids in bed. In those long months of study, I learned a few things. I discovered that the people in the Bible were just ordinary. Some were good, some were bad. Most could be categorized somewhere in between. But I also discerned that God constituted a real part of their lives. They acknowledged Him as alive, personal, and involved in what they did, even when they chose to ignore Him.

I knew God played no part in my life. After months of consideration, Janet and I took action. We began to attend a church and listen to what they told us. We'd arrive a little late, sit in the back, and leave early. Hardly anyone knew we were there.

I soon realized that being a Christian meant more than assenting to a philosophical system. It required face-to-face confrontation with a Person who lives and loves, rules and reigns, provides for and protects all who believe in Him. I also discovered that belief in Jesus Christ wasn't unreasonable. It required a step of faith, but healthy evidence supported that step. The more I learned, the more convinced I became that the whole matter made sense. In fact, once I had accepted Jesus for who He was, all creation made sense. World history made sense. My family life made sense. In short, a door opened to the possibility that I could now attain the quality life that had escaped me before.

I'm still working at understanding, complying with, and enjoying this relationship with God. But the missing piece has been found.

Take time to consider your own spiritual commitment. It might need a renewal. It might need to be acknowledged for the first time. Or you could read the rest of this book and skip all that. But sooner or later, you'll be caught with one of your boundary markers down. When that happens, you'll have no clear definition of what you're trying to build. You'll still be aimless and frustrated.

"Follow the tongue" was a phrase of the Old West. When hunters, trappers, and pioneers first barged into the wastelands, no roads gave them their bearings. They simply headed West. Without road signs, maps, and friendly gas station attendants, how did they find their way? How could they make sure they rode west?

They solved that problem by reading the stars at night, locating the north star, and then pointing the tongue of their wagon due west. Next morning the stars faded from sight. All they needed to do was "follow the tongue."

That's just what Jesus Christ can do for your family. He can be your North Star, the constant guidepost to keep you on course. No matter how many times you have or haven't considered Him, you must continually come back to that basic relationship with Him.

What does a winning family look like? That's difficult to say, because quality comes in different sizes and shapes and shades for each family. Each must find for themselves what fits best. Let me give you a glimpse of how it works for us.

Last Saturday my oldest son, Russell, and his wife, Lois, stopped by to borrow a tool. I suggested they stay for dinner. My wife, Janet, picked up on the idea and started fixing a salad. Lois chipped in to help with dessert. I fired up the grill for the meat. Russell engaged in a lively conversation about cars with his eighteen-year-old brother, Mike.

Our youngest, Aaron, age five, pestered the big brothers until they kicked the soccer ball around with him.

We sat down to eat our simple meal. Nothing gourmet. The furnishings were webbed-patio style. The view, a neighbor's cement block wall, was less than inspiring. But the contentment was there.

We're a family who enjoys themselves. We like to be with each other. The kids treat Mom with respect and trust that Dad will have a piece of wisdom worth listening to once in a while.

A warm spring evening and a dish of homemade ice cream. No TV blaring. No hostile remarks. Just six common people kicked back and enjoying life together.

Pure quality.

I'm convinced that's what family life's meant to be.

It's part of the reward of working to build a family that's a winner.

2

Caring Dads Wear Cowboy Hats

Christie stared at the doorway of my office. Her eyes opened wider, her chin dropped. Engrossed in my reading, I didn't notice her at first. It was Friday afternoon, usually my day off. But Christie had called the day before to ask a favor. We had never met but knew a mutual friend. I agreed to meet her at the office to answer some questions. Now I suspected this young lady from the east coast had been caught by surprise.

I sat at my desk, leaned back in my chair, my old cowboy boots propped up on one corner near the phone. Attired in blue jeans and Western long-sleeved shirt, I admit to being a little grubbier than usual. I'd just got back from riding a horse in the hills. Since it was spring, the horse was shedding. My pants looked like wooly chaps. I had *Trails Plowed Under*, a book written by turn-of-the-century Western artist Charles Russell, propped in my hand. From a stereo headset perched on my head Merle Haggard wailed, "Big city, turn me loose and set me free, somewhere in the middle of Montana."

Christie peeled her eyes from me and examined my office. Against the wall, a poster displays artifacts from the Winchester Gun Museum of Cody, Wyoming. A prized photograph of downtown Ogden, Utah, taken in 1870, a hat rack holding my brown Stetson, and about a dozen Russell prints are scattered around the bookcase. An old cowpoke statue decorates my coffee table. On my desk sits a five-pound hunk of iron pyrite and a magnificent handmade reproduction of Lewis and Clark's one and only compass.

But I think Thunder startled her most. Thunder is a four-foot stuffed buffalo that hangs from the ceiling next to the east window. I didn't know how many pastor's offices she'd stepped into before, but I don't think she expected this.

"Are you—the reverend?" she stammered.

"Yep," I smiled.

"Oh! Well, I've heard all about you—I think!"

Reactions like that happen to me all the time. The old cowboy hat and I have taken second glances at pastors' conferences, in Europe, in the Mideast, in New York City, and West Palm Beach. From coast to coast we've traveled together. But I wouldn't want you to think I wear that old hat everywhere. When I dress up I wear the new gray Stetson.

Boots, jeans, cowboy hat—that's me. I grew up wearing Roy Rogers pajamas and firing cap guns at the neighborhood alley cats.

Caring dads wear cowboy hats.

Within God's freedom, we can be ourselves. Paul put it this way: "The faith which you have, have as your own conviction before God. Happy is he who does not condemn himself in what he approves" (Romans 14:22).

You and I have freedom. We do not have the freedom, as caring dads, to be sinful, unbiblical, or purposely offensive. But we can allow our unique expression out. For me, this translates into leather belts with my name on the back and silver buckles. For you it might mean something entirely different. I have no intention of converting the world to my style of dress. However, I'm pleased to find myself a healthy additive for my whole family.

One of the most common complaints parents make about children is the adage, "The kids are always giving in to peer pressure. I wish they'd stand on their own." One obvious area is the way kids dress. Dads lament, "Why do they have to dress like that?"

And why not? What example do they follow? Mom and Dad dress just like their peers. They imitate different peers, that's all. Both parents and children conform to what they think those around them expect.

So if a dad comes along who breaks out of the mold and wears what he feels comfortable wearing, what does that tell the children? It doesn't necessarily convince them to dress like Dad. Neither of my older boys wear boots or hats. But they've each found their own style, regardless of the latest fads.

That doesn't mean you have to find some different garb just to prove your point, either. You don't have to be a shadow rider. That's what they called the man in the Old West who liked his clothes so much he constantly looked at the shadow he cast. But you do need to let your family know that you make decisions apart from peer pressure. That's a living model for them to do the same.

Thoughtless conformity shows up in our speech, too. I'm thinking more of vocabulary than dialect.

Our dialect frames the rich heritage we acquire from our early environment. What a diversity we enjoy within the American inflections. The man from New York City stands out from the guy who hails from Winston-Salem, North Carolina, who in turn distinguishes himself from the Texan. Even we native Californians bear accents.

It's not the dialect that hampers us but our vocabulary. "Listen to my child talk," we may groan. "She tries so hard to sound like everybody else."

A few years ago teens in our area were invaded by the "valley girl" talk. It was, to say the least, totally awesome. I spend most of my days working with words one way or another, so to find a new vocabulary is a refreshing and creative change. The point is, our words should communicate the message we want to get across. We should choose words and phrases that are our own.

Most of us dads exist in a private world of jargon. A common language provides acceptance and even helps advance careers. Preachers can be guilty too. During a recent backyard tirade directed at my five-year-old about the evils of leaving one's sweater on the swing during a rainstorm, I crescendoed to a convicting conclusion. Whereby Aaron beamed and said, "Amen and Amen." He was greatly relieved to have the sermon over.

I know I need to work at cultivating a vocabulary with integrity— one that's an honest reflection of me. As a graduate student in philosophy, I spent years learning a phony language supposed to impress scholastic deep thinkers. Three years at seminary taught me to sound like a theological journal.

I think I've made the transition back to the real me. A British magazine recently asked permission to reprint one of my articles. They also wanted approval to "change the word 'yup' on page 2, paragraph 4, to read 'yes.' "

Did I let them change the word?

Yup.

Your children don't have to use your ways of expression, but they need to be encouraged to build their own creative, imaginative vocabulary.

We need to watch our eating habits too. One dad told me at a recent men's barbecue that he couldn't get his son to eat and drink anything but cheeseburgers and root beer. "No matter how fancy the restaurant, his order's the same." A few weeks later I mentioned our conversation to Jeff, his son. He remarked, "Well, did he tell you what he orders? A steak, medium rare, a green salad with blue cheese dressing, and a baked potato with nothing on it. You can count on it."

Getting the picture? We teach our children independence. We teach them to discover their own uniqueness. We teach them they have freedom to be themselves. Meanwhile, they're watching us.

Take time to notice the music you listen to, the books you read, the television you watch, the possessions you long for, even how you spend your leisure time. If you find yourself in ruts that are attempts to conform to someone else's image, then your children may do the same.

Use the following exercise to get a better handle on your own struggle with peer pressure. Take time to answer the questions on a sheet of paper and answer them as if you had no worries about what others would think or say.

1. What three pieces of clothing would I like to buy to make a clearer statement of who I am?

2. According to a survey of my family, what are the most over-

worked words and phrases in my vocabulary? What could I substitute for these words or phrases and still maintain my integrity and clarity?

3. What is my favorite type of food? What are some dishes I've never tried? (Make a commitment to try two of these within the next few weeks. Set a deadline.)

4. How would I classify the kind of music I listen to most? Even if nobody knew what I listened to, would I still listen to this type of music? (If yes, give three good reasons why you listen to this type of music. Within the next week make sure everyone in your family understands why you choose to listen to this music.)

5. What are the last three books I've read? What could an outsider, looking at these titles and descriptions, learn about me? Would their observations be an accurate picture of who I am? If not, then what kind of books would give them a clearer picture?

6. Approximately how many hours a week do I spend watching TV? In my opinion, is this too much, not enough, or about right? What type of programs would my children say I usually watch? In what way do these programs help promote my image of who I really am?

7. If I had $1,000 to spend on myself, what would I probably buy? How does this item fit into my life-style, that is, how I see myself to be?

8. If I had two free hours to myself, what would I like to do? If I had a whole day to myself, what would I like to do? If I had three days to myself, what would I like to do?

Some sincere Christian dads hold back from expressing their uniqueness because they fear they might, in biblical terms, "cause a brother to stumble." This is an important fact to consider. Romans 14:13 states this principle.

However, Paul is warning us here not to do anything to weaken the faith of another. I have found, for instance, that my wearing a cowboy hat weakens no one's faith. True, some people don't care for the way I dress, but they don't feel their relationship with God threatened by it. In an extreme case, someone might judge by my casual manner that my faith is weak (something Paul cautions about in the same verse). But this doesn't threaten their own personal faith.

A second caution in being yourself is sensitivity in not offending those important people in your life. Your favorite clothes might include a dingy, torn green sweater that your wife abhors.

But I've found that once your family has worked through understanding your style, they accept the peripheries more readily. How does my wife tolerate my wearing jeans? Simple. I dress as nicely as I can to please her, in the style that pleases me.

The living proof of our own freedom is a much stronger message to our kids than a hundred lectures. How can we do that?

Be consistent. For many men it's hard to be yourself because you haven't yet discovered who you are. Whole careers flash by, and energies are spent without taking time to find out your true self.

We have to work at shucking the image of others. Once you discover and identify areas of change, stick to the new image. You'll never convince anyone else to break out of peer pressure if you're dissuaded to take the risk yourself.

Be reasonable. You should be able to explain to others why you do the things you do. I wear Western shirts because their double yokes make them longer lasting than other shirts, they never go out of style, and because it helps people remember me.

Be tolerant. If you expect others to accept your individuality, you'll need to reciprocate.

My son Mike marched to the breakfast table on school-picture day with his "Renounce The World!" black T-shirt on. Now, granted, that's a very biblical statement. But I was thinking something a little more "preppy" would look nice for his photo. But I didn't make him change. He wasn't being sinful, or even sloppy. He was just being Mike.

I walked to the back of the sanctuary of the large church on the closing night of a Family Living Conference. A line of friendly folks waited to respond to my talk about dads. As the crowd thinned, a few more serious people stepped forward. They spoke of tense family struggles and asked how to apply certain principles to themselves. We talked, we prayed, even cried. Then I prepared to leave.

One last man stood by the coat rack. I picked up my Stetson, and he walked with me out into the chilly February night.

"I've got to admit," he said, "I've wanted to wear one of those cowboy hats for almost forty years now, but, well, you know—what would people say?"

"What kind of work do you do?" I asked.

"A veterinarian—small animals though." He sounded apologetic.

"Would wearing a cowboy hat to and from your office interfere with the quality of your work?" I inquired.

"No—it's, well, I'm afraid I'd stand out in a crowd."

"Only for the first three minutes," I assured him. "A good hat'll cost you about a hundred dollars. That's a lot of money for a toy that's only used at yearly costume parties. But if you do buy one and wear it every day for three months, I'll guarantee you won't ever want to stop wearing one. Don't spend another forty years failing to do a simple thing like wearing a cowboy hat."

A couple weeks later I got a note from the man. "Two things have happened since the conference. I bought a cowboy hat and am wearing it. And my sixteen-year-old daughter's decided to dress like a punk rocker. Talk about a weird household. What should I do now?"

I wrote back this note: "Peter . . . hang in there. Be consistent. Be reasonable. And be tolerant."

Four months passed, and I got another note. Peter announced: "Last week my daughter decided that if I would give up wearing my cowboy hat, she'd change her hair and dress style too. But I told her no. I explained that I liked my hat because it was warm, comfortable, and distinctive. I told her I wore it because it fit who I saw myself to be. Well, yesterday she had her hair back to normal and wore civilized clothes. She told me she was tired of a hairdo that hurt every night when she slept and makeup that made her look like she had one foot in the grave. I was shocked at the change since I'd never given her a lecture on the subject."

I wasn't shocked. He proved something I've known all along—caring dads wear cowboy hats.

3

Caring Dads Build Phone Book Holders

Janet was bushed. And she had every reason to be. It was our eighteenth move in twenty years of marriage.

Way back when she said "I do," she had no idea she'd married a restless pioneer who'd drag her through countless adventures. Now our brand new house in the woods of north Idaho brimmed with boxes of belongings. Janet stood and stared in the kitchen. Having fewer kitchen cupboards would challenge her expertise in unpacking.

Meanwhile, I threw myself into the important project of building a cover for the back porch. I cut beams, leveled rafters, and installed fiberglass sheeting in preparation to paint. It seemed quite reasonable that I should work on the porch and she would put away the dishes and utensils.

At noon I was surprised to find her still staring, nothing put away. "I just don't know where to begin," she moaned.

By midafternoon I was hanging onto a rafter with hammer in hand and nail in mouth when she appeared at the door. She displayed the first real smile since we'd left southern California. "Hey, do you know what I need?" she asked, grinning.

"What?" I mumbled.

"I need a phone book holder."

I spit some nails from my mouth. "A what?"

She shaded the sun from her eyes and explained: "If I had a little desk top to go on the counter under the wall phone, I could put the phone book underneath and my calendar on top. Then I'd get the whole kitchen organized."

Her suggestion sounded ludicrous. Stop my important project for something so trivial?

"Oh, I know you're busy," she continued, "but I do think it would look nice in brown." Then she disappeared inside.

I quickly dismissed the whole subject and got back to my job. Then something caught my eye. Right down there on the ground, next to the nail bucket, lay a small scrap of plywood. As I hammered I began to envision how it could be ripped to make a small rustic desk top for the phone book. Before I realized it, I had stepped down to begin. I painted it with dark brown latex and left it to dry in the warm summer breeze.

We rummaged through the boxes for dishes for dinner that night. Later I presented my completed project. "Here it is," I announced, as though I was a sculptor unveiling his latest creation, "one genuine-north-Idaho-rustic-mini-desktop-phone-book holder."

"Wow, that's great." She beamed. "But, you didn't have to do that—I mean, you had so much other—" she bubbled as she placed the prize in its honored position.

"Well, what do you think?" I prodded.

"I think . . . " She paused to throw her arms around me. "I think you must love your wife very much."

Enjoying this unexpected reward, I asked, "What makes you say that?"

"Because you had plenty of excuses not to do it, and yet you thought enough of me to stop everything else and do this. Now I can take care of the kitchen—"

By bedtime the kitchen gear was unpacked and put away.

Loving deeds.

One simple, loving deed.

Caring dads need to cram their lives with them.

"Let us not love with word or with tongue, but in deed and truth" (1 John 3:18). John is not saying that we should never utter "I love yous" to our wives or children. He's saying we need a love so sincere that it reveals itself in action as well as words.

True love shows gentleness, kindness, compassion, and concern to another without any thought of what we receive in return. It's an act of the will, not solely a feeling. We decide whom to love and how to demonstrate that love.

God didn't hesitate to give us an open, tangible demonstration of His love. Even to the spiritually dense, He continues to display His love in the beauty of creation and the bounty of this earth. We're reminded in Matthew 5:45 that "He causes His sun to rise on the evil and the good, and sends rain on the righteous and the unrighteous."

The spectacular sparkle of ocean sunsets, the delicate fragrance of alpine flowers, the peaceful serenity of young deer grazing in meadows hint to our confused world of the love of its Creator.

God's love pours out even more clearly through His love letter to us. I believe every Christian would thrill to have God speak audibly, "I love you." At first we would explode with joy at this personal touch. But sooner or later we'd crave more assurances. Maybe we have a lousy month; maybe we make some mistakes, or His words fade till they seem like a dream. Does He still love us?

To avoid such problems, God gave us written words to constantly remind us of His continuing acceptance and concern. Verse after verse, chapter after chapter, book after book, the message repeats His primary concern to make friends with mankind, to allow them to experience the power of His love.

But the Bible is more than just words. God understands our need for loving deeds. Paul records God's ultimate expression of love to mankind: "But God demonstrates His own love toward us, in that while we were yet sinners, Christ died for us" (Romans 5:8).

That's what love's all about. Not merely nice, sweet words but concrete actions that prove the worth of those words.

Here are some suggestions that can help to keep our loving deeds on track.

First, a loving feeling isn't required to do a loving act.

I heard the footsteps coming down the hall, and I knew what the first word would be. The whole family slept except me and one other. "Daddy!" a small voice cried out in the night. "Daddy, come quick. I barfed all over Paws, and I think he's going to die."

Michael was only five at the time, but his natural affection for animals made his bed the nocturnal resting place for the family cat, Paws. I struggled to my feet and staggered down the hallway, hoping I'd heard wrong. Perhaps Michael had been dreaming.

No such luck.

The previous evening's pizza and popcorn had not set well with Michael's sensitive stomach. Now the cat streaked, panic stricken, through the house. There was a little boy to wash up and comfort, a bed to change, a bedspread and sheets to launder, a trail through the house to clean up, and a very angry and frightened cat to capture.

I've never enjoyed giving cats a bath—even in the bright light of a warm spring day. Standing on the back porch in my pajamas at 3:45 A.M., on a cold linoleum floor, next to a tearful son, trying to coax a smelly cat to dip himself into some suds isn't on my list of delightful things to do.

All three of us survived, and except for one nasty scratch on my left hand everything turned out fine. By daylight I tumbled back to bed just as Janet rolled over and yawned. "What did Mike need, a hug?"

"Yeah, something like that," I muttered.

It was a loving act, without any particular loving feeling.

Second, look for motive-free acts of love. The most vivid demonstrations of our love for others are always those things we do that we don't have to do.

Suppose your wife hints that you really ought to do something about cleaning up the backyard. You've been too busy with overtime at the office and coaching Little League every Saturday. But finally you spend one whole day breaking your back to get the place slicked up.

That evening you collapse in your favorite chair. Your wife's on the couch across the room, and a baseball game blasts from the TV. At an appropriate moment (such as a replay of the most incredible catch of the season), she says, "You should see the beautiful roses that David sent to Cynthia today. They make her house look so elegant." Then there's a well-timed pause. "When was the last time you bought me roses?"

"Roses!" you boom. "Roses!" Dave slows down at an intersection, buys some posies from a vendor, and his wife's in seventh heaven. You break your back all day in the yard and don't even get some sympathy for your strained muscles.

The difference in the actions is often the motive behind them. You cleaned the yard for two primary reasons. One, you couldn't find your five iron that Junior said he left in the backyard somewhere, and the company's tournament is coming up. Two, your boss and his wife are coming over for a barbecue next Friday night, and you're not about to let them see the yard in that mess.

The flowers, however, came to Cynthia as a spur of the moment idea that said, "I was thinking about you and wanted to do something extraordinary to say 'I love you.' "

Both acts are appreciated. But only one is long cherished and remembered.

Third, loving deeds should be a habit, not an exception.

In all my years of sitting across the desk from couples with marriage problems, I've never once found a woman whose problem was that her husband did too many loving deeds for her. Sometimes a husband equates buying objects with loving deeds and then can't understand his wife's dissatisfaction. "But I buy her everything she wants," he complains.

True loving deeds, that is, giving to the other without expecting anything in return, are so rare in marriage that most wives can remember every instance in which they ever happened.

"I remember the time he stayed up until two thirty helping me complete those crazy Christmas decorations. Then he let me sleep in and fixed breakfast for the kids."

Why is it she remembers that incident? Because it stands out there alone in a world sparse of loving deeds.

I sat on the fence of the corral and watched Krissie come out to the stables to care for her horse, Jake. Krissie comes out twice a day, as she has for twelve years now. That afternoon I watched her comb and brush the chocolate-brown gelding. Then she hosed him down, washed around his eyes, brushed him again, and toweled him off.

She lifted each hoof for inspection and scraped out the mud and

rocks. She fed him sweet oats, tied him to the rail, and cleaned out
his stall, scattering it with fresh straw. She sprayed him all over with
fly spray, put a head stall on him, and led him down the lane to the
other stables. Krissie says Jake always likes to see the other horses.
When they returned to the corral, she filled up his water trough,
tossed an old volleyball in the water for him to play with, gave him a
hug, and closed the gate.

"Aren't you going to ride?" I asked.

"No, I don't have time today." She smiled.

She does the same thing everyday, whether she rides Jake or not.
Krissie makes a habit of showing loving deeds to that sixteen-hand
quarter horse. You and I can build habits like that too.

Fourth, the world knows our love for our family by the deeds in
public, not the words whispered in private.

Lydia and Frank sat next to each other across from my office desk.
It was the typical first counseling session before separation. The pattern often seems to be: wait until you're convinced that this session
will do no good, then make your token trip to the pastor so you can
tell others, "Well, we tried counseling." It makes me feel like a relief
pitcher in baseball who's brought in to finish the game after the
team's already lost.

I looked right at Frank. "Do you love Lydia?"

He stammered, cleared his throat, and shrugged. I wasn't sure
what that meant.

"Frank," I repeated, "I didn't catch that. Do you love Lydia?"

"Well, it's—I mean, we've never—it's hard to—"

He tried to explain the message with a wave of his arms.

"Frank, if you were suddenly at the gates of heaven, and St. Peter
handed you a short quiz with one question, 'Do you love Lydia?' and
the only answer could be yes or no, which would you reply?"

Frank looked at his shoes, hesitated, then said, "Yes."

"Then you do love Lydia?" I prompted.

"Yeah," he acknowledged.

"Then I'd like you to turn to Lydia and tell her that."

"What?" he said, squirming.

"You just admitted that you love her. So how about turning, looking her in the eye, and saying, 'Lydia, I love you.' "

For a moment I expected him to get up and walk out the door.

Instead, he turned towards his brunette wife, still looking at his feet, then glanced quickly at her face and rapidly muttered, "I love you." Then he turned back to face me.

We talked together for forty-five more minutes, and they got up to leave. Lydia hung back to speak to me alone. "I know it didn't seem like much, but do you know that was the first time in seventeen years that Frank said or did anything in public to show he cared about me? I mean, there was the 'I do' and the kiss at the wedding, and that was it."

Sometime I'd like to tell you how Frank and Lydia solved their differences. Maybe someday I can. Right now I can't say how things are going because Frank moved to San Diego, and Lydia's in Phoenix. Seventeen years of misunderstanding, selfishness, and petty quarrels are not easily undone. There are no easy answers. But I can't help wondering what their status would be today if Frank had learned early to express his love for Lydia in public words and deeds.

Listen to the ways other men talk about their wives in public. Watch how they treat them when others are around. Are there lots of jokes at the wives' expense? Or unkind cuts? Or do they show love and respect through praise and appreciation? We can learn from both the positive and negative models.

Fifth, true love works off her things-to-do list.

I don't know where they learn it. Maybe it's one of those things passed down on Grandma's knee. But every woman I know carries a projects-to-do-around-the-house list. She might call it her "jobs jar" or her "honey-do list" or "Daddy's duties," but it all comes out the same.

The list always has some items that you can agree need your attention. But then there are always those few about which you're convinced she doesn't understand the complexity of the problem or the time and expense involved. Yet there's little you can do to more deeply express your love for her than to grab up that list and complete at least some of the projects.

I have two suggestions. Pick an item that's her original idea. If it's a pet project of yours, she might not understand the love attached to it. Then complete the job you begin. The only thing worse than having no job done is having dozens of jobs half done.

Like most guys I know, I enjoy fixing up the house and keeping up on the chores. But I don't always have the time for it. Days off are rare for me. When I do have time at home, I like to play with Aaron, our youngest, or collapse in an easy chair.

This month's been a hectic time of travel, speaking, writing, and pastoring. Last Tuesday, as I trekked off to work, a neat little list lay on the counter next to my keys.

Jobs To Do:

a) Fix back door (it won't lock at night)
b) Fix towel rack in boys' bathroom (it fell down again)
c) Fix dining room curtains (I can't get them to open)

It was signed "Jan," and there was the familiar accompanying happy face.

Since we'd survived several months with these same problems, I assumed we could get by a while longer. But as I drove to the office, I realized that my life was always this hectic. There was never a good time to stop and do chores. Today was as good as any other.

On my way home for lunch, I picked up a new door handle and a couple of bolts for the towel rack. By one o'clock the back door was secure and the towel rack able to withstand the Tarzan leap of a five-year-old. Then I tackled the curtains in the dining room. It turned out to be a simpler job than I imagined.

Janet helped me hold the curtains as I worked the drawstring. "I think this is one of those times when I'd better stay out of the room until you're finished," she suggested.

Her caution reminded me of my reputation for intensity when involved with the frustrations of mechanical breakdowns. But I summoned up a cheerful laugh. "Stick around, it's no big thing," I said. And for once it wasn't.

By 1:29 P.M., I had finished the chores on her list.

"I've got one of the good ones," Jan said, grinning.

I wasn't about to tell her otherwise. You'd be surprised how much love is communicated by working from her things-to-do list.

Sixth, expressing love requires creativity. A creative expression of love says, "I spent time thinking about you." That doesn't mean we neglect the routine expressions.

It was the Brittons' twentieth anniversary. Lloyd wanted to say something special to Louise. He told her, "Friday, right after work, let's go out to dinner. Some place real nice."

Louise complained that 5:00 P.M. was a little early for a fancy restaurant, but Lloyd insisted. Even though she prodded him, Lloyd refused to disclose their destination. Louise was startled when they drove into the Burbank airport.

"We're taking a little trip," Lloyd announced. A shocked Louise boarded a jet to San Francisco. By 8:30 they were seated in a plush restaurant at the top of one of San Francisco's finest hotels. It was a beautiful, romantic evening complete with dinner, plenty of laughing, and a red-eye special home.

They arrived home by 2:30 A.M.

Not every budget could withstand that type of display. But the celebration demonstrated to Louise a lot of love. She knew that Lloyd had to watch the papers for the airfare wars and buy the tickets a month ahead of time for the discounts. She knew he had to arrange for transportation and restaurant reservations. And she knew that he had to hide it all from her for a long time in order to carry off such a big surprise.

I fully expect Lloyd and Louise to have many more anniversaries. Somewhere down the road they may forget many of the yearly events. But I don't think they'll ever forget that dinner in San Francisco.

Creative love can mean a late night summer picnic on the beach or a rented limousine. The important thing is the message that rings out, "I love you so much I've been scheming for ways to show you."

Seventh, loving deeds personally stretch you. Someone might comment, "If I spent all my time running around doing loving deeds, I wouldn't have time for anything else." But, I wonder, what is the alternative? Doing unloving deeds?

The more we purposely show love to others, the more we're changed. Those around us benefit from receiving the act; we benefit from the emotional, social, and spiritual maturity that comes to us by doing it. Therefore, to cause the most character growth in our own lives, we need to pick out some loving deeds that won't be easy to complete.

Last June, my wife and five-year-old traveled to northern Idaho to stay the summer. I planned to join them in August. That meant a separation of six weeks. Even though we'd been married twenty-two years, six weeks sounded like a very long time. We set up a time twice a week to call, and I promised to write.

Some people are prolific letter writers. I'm not. I'm more the quick-phone-call-and-get-right-to-the-point type of person. But I determined to write often to Janet. In fact, before she left, I secretly decided that I'd write her a brief note everyday.

The day we parted I began my first letter, and that began my daily routine. There wasn't always a lot to say.

By the second week I realized what a chore I'd taken on. Then I hit on a solution to help me keep going with my goal. I announced to my congregation on Sunday that I wanted to write to Janet every day and asked that they check up on me.

There was no way to back off. By the fourth week the habit was so ingrained that I looked forward to the morning ritual.

Caring dads do loving deeds.

We all know that.

Will loving deeds guarantee a perfect family? There's no promise of that. But it's hard to imagine any real contentment without them.

4

Caring Dads Sing Solos

Don't you just love small churches?

I do.

When we lived in northern Idaho, my wife and I wrote full time. On weekends I pastored the tiny town's only Protestant church. We had a membership of about forty-five people. Attendance each Sunday ranged as high as seventy-five or eighty. We even had a choir, though it often resembled a women's ensemble. On occasion we'd pick up a couple of male voices.

In order to insure my humility, I suppose, the Lord chose not to give me musical talent. My singing ability, after many years of practice, still borders the disaster zone. It's a common joke that I've been begged by my congregation to keep preaching so they wouldn't have to hear my singing.

One Sunday morning I tried to think of some way to encourage the men in our congregation to come to choir practice. Finally, I blurted out in the service, "If we can have four men singing in the choir next week, I'll sing a solo in church."

After church several of the fellows assured me they'd be there. As it turned out, not one man showed up. Actually, I was relieved. The spur-of-the-moment promise had unnerved me.

A few weeks later we had no choir or special music of any kind. It was harvest time, so neither the men or women had time for choir.

During the singing of a hymn, I had a brainstorm for livening up our worship. Since the front of the church was a large, open space, I called the entire right half of the congregation—about twenty-five people—to come up front. I instructed them to be our spontaneous choir and sing a hymn. Men, women, and children filed up and sang.

Then I asked the left half of the congregation to come sing. Everyone seemed to enjoy their participation. After the second "choir" sat down, my wife stood up.

"Pastor," she said. I knew I was in some kind of trouble right away. My wife rarely speaks up in church, and she never calls me "pastor." "Pastor," she repeated, "I believe there were more than four men in the choir today. I believe you owe us a solo."

Everyone whooped, hollered, and clapped. I knew I was stuck. So the next Sunday, knees knocking and voice cracking, with sweaty palms and nervous stomach, I sang my first solo in church. The reason I followed through with it was simple: I knew I had to be a man of my word.

Caring dads always keep their word.

Jesus instructed: "But let your statement be, 'Yes, yes' or 'No, no'; and anything beyond these is of evil" (Matthew 5:37).

In biblical times a man's word measured his reputation and worth. The very words a man spoke described him as much as did his head, hands, and body. Promises were not to be broken.

Isaac, an old and nearly blind man, couldn't see Jacob, his youngest son, when he came to receive a blessing. Jacob deceived his father into thinking he was the elder son, Esau, and Isaac gave Jacob the eldest son's blessing.

When the deception was exposed, Esau tried to get his father to retract his blessing to Jacob. Isaac refused. He'd spoken the words; he had to be true to his word.

What a far cry from today's world. We no longer expect a man's word to be true—we want to see it in writing. Even then, we want a lawyer to examine the contract before we sign. Later, if we really want out of the agreement, even contracts can be disregarded.

It wasn't always that way. I grew up on the farms and ranches of the American West. There was, when I was young, still the faint glimmer of something called the Code of the West. An unwritten set of rules and standards bound men of integrity in frontier America, long before laws or lawmen regulated actions. The code included the axiom: A man's only as good as his word. Here's how it worked.

In the early 1870s a man by the name of Andrew Garcia left Bozeman, Montana, to hunt buffalo. Buffalo hides provided a valuable trading commodity. A skilled trader who persevered could make good money.

Garcia needed to borrow some money from a man in Bozeman to get his start. He needed a string of pack horses and some proper gear. He told his lender he expected to return from the Yellowstone region within three months to pay him back. His promise entailed his word and a handshake.

Garcia was a tough man, but the winter proved tougher. Early snowstorms, Indian trouble, and the unpredictable buffalo themselves kept Garcia up in the mountains well over a year. By the time he completed his hunt, he had veered south and would have a long, arduous journey back to Bozeman.

Some acquaintances told him to forget the merchant. After all, the man would have considered him a business loss by now. And there was no way he could pursue Garcia to retrieve his investment. Garcia insisted he had a debt to pay. He trudged hundreds of miles north. A man of his word.

Garcia is not an isolated instance. Many men followed this rule. But today it stands out because it's no longer the rule but the exception.

Promises concern business deals and families too. Caring dads keep small promises and major ones. They are known to their loved ones as men of their word.

We all have reasons for breaking a promise. Perhaps that's a good sign. At least it reveals that somewhere deep inside we feel the need to justify going back on our word. Most excuses fit into one of the following categories.

Cheap promises. Accenting a statement with "I promise" implies that this statement is more valid than an ordinary statement, which defeats itself. All of our words should ring true.

The quick vacation stop at Great-aunt Sarah's bombed. Wayne and his family hadn't seen her in fifteen years. She barely remembered who he was. She didn't like children in her tiny urban apartment, even though six cats roamed her living room. Her two Siamese spent the entire forty-five minute visit scratching little Dawn, who finally hit one with a pillow.

Heading out the door, Wayne attempted to urge his family on and calm Aunt Sarah. Trying to think of something civil to say, he stammered, "Hey, I'll tell Grandma to write and give you that pecan pie recipe we talked about."

She brightened up. "You do that, and don't forget the next time you come to the city to see your Auntie Sarah more often. Promise?"

"Oh, I promise, Aunt Sarah," Wayne mumbled as he brushed her cheek with a kiss.

Out on the freeway, Dawn cried. "Daddy, I don't ever want to go there again. The cats are mean. The house smells funny, and I couldn't even sit down without Aunt Sarah yelling at me. Why do we have to go back?"

"We don't have to go back," Wayne informed her.

"Yes we do," Dawn sobbed. "You promised."

"Oh, no." Wayne tried to explain. "We were just talking. It was just conversation—not like a real promise. You know what I mean?"

Dawn didn't. All she learned was that a promise isn't always a promise. Now she would wonder in the future whether Dad's promises to her were real ones or imitation ones.

Caring dads watch their words.

Undefined priorites. It's common to give in to the most current pressure upon us.

One night I planned a relaxing evening at home. That's a rare treat for me, so I told my wife we'd do something special together. But just before noon, Don called to ask if he could stop by that evening to talk over some committee plans. I agreed.

When I reached the house at 5:00 P.M., Aaron had a note from his teacher asking Jan and me to attend a special parents' advisory committee meeting at the school. It was a project we both wanted to be involved in, so I called Don to cancel out with him.

We were almost out the door when the police called to say that the back door of the church stood open. They wanted me to come right down to see if anything had been stolen. So Janet went to the school meeting. I looked over the church. Three promises—one to Jan, one to Don, and one to the school—had all been broken. All I had to show for the evening was one satisfied policeman.

I felt frustrated. My life wasn't in control. I was being pushed about by the latest pressure. How could I have made my word good?

I could have told Don I was tied up for the evening and met him for breakfast instead. I could have written a note to the teacher to tell her we were very interested in the advisory meeting but needed more than a few hour's notice. I could have told the police to close the door, that later the janitor or I would come down to check the church.

I could have been a man of my word if I had had a clearer sense of the important things as well as the urgent things.

Promises that manipulate. Sometimes we renege on our word because we've used it as merely a tool for our own motives. We're thinking only of today, without showing much concern for the future.

For instance, we'll say, "Honey, I don't think I'll get started cleaning the garage like I mentioned because it's such a big job, and I couldn't possibly finish it in one day. What if I wait for a three-day weekend? Oh, by the way, did I tell you Tom's stopping by? He wants me to go play racquetball this evening."

So we've broken our original word and also thrown out an ambiguous implication that sometime in the future we'll get that garage cleaned. Two purposes have been accomplished. One, it's hoped the wife is appeased and won't keep nagging. Two, we've got lots of time to weasel out of it next time too.

In this instance, the words we say aren't statements of fact, nor are they desires of our hearts. They're weapons for controlling the present situation in our favor.

Insensitivity. "I didn't know it meant that much to you!" Have you ever had to say that to a tearful wife or child?

On Monday Linda asked Alan to take her shopping at the Hacienda Mall the following Friday evening. "Sounds great," he said, smiling.

Linda loved to shop, and Alan loved to have Linda in a good mood. So no problem—until Ernie came by Friday afternoon to tell Alan about his new bass fishing boat.

"Come out with me after work. I'm going to give it a trial run on the lake," Ernie announced.

"Sure thing," Alan agreed. After all, the only thing he had planned was a shopping trip. That could wait.

Alan called Linda from the lake marina. "I'll be home a little after dark—I didn't want you to worry about me."

Meanwhile, Linda, after spending an active week cooped up in the house with two preschoolers, had just bathed, fed, and shuffled the kids off to the neighbors. All week she'd looked forward to the shopping trip—not really because she wanted to buy anything, but because she wanted out of the house for a few hours. She wanted to be alone with Alan. She wanted them to dream together about some furniture they might buy some day.

When Linda lets out a shriek, Alan is dumbfounded. "What's the big deal? I'll take you shopping in the morning."

Each word sails across the phone wires like a dart.

"Hey, no problem. We can take the kids with us." By now, Alan is impatient to get into that boat. "Even better than that—tell me what you want, anything—I'll pick it up for you on the way home."

Alan stares at the phone as it clicks. "Surely it didn't mean that much to her—?"

Caring dads sense the value of their words to the people around them.

Forgetfulness. "But, Daddy, you promised!"

"Yeah, I know, but that was before I saw what this day was going to be like. I forgot all about picking up your jacket at the cleaners because the company controller came in this morning. He went over all the new accounts. Then, this afternoon the Chicago branch called. Said they hadn't received the overnight express mail. We had to give them the whole business over the phone. Plus, Stu Weinert decided to take a job with Lodge Brothers. Suddenly we had to re-staff next week's schedule. By the time I hit the car all I could think about was getting home, kicking off my shoes, and relaxing. You understand, don't you?"

Tami hangs her head. "Sure, I understand. I'm just not important enough to remember."

We can chalk it up to hectic life-styles, job stress, unexpected circumstances, or information overload. But it translates the same to those on the other side.

Laziness. Mike, our middle son, is about 1,100 miles away at college. Every once in awhile he gets a hankering for some home cooking. He and I used to spend some time in the kitchen baking up batches of cookies, so it seemed natural for me to pick up a package of chocolate chips with the thought of sending him a tin full of munchies.

I mentioned to him during our weekly Sunday night phone call that some cookies would be on their way. But the chocolate chips are still in the freezer. I could have made them Saturday, but the playoffs were on TV. Then Sunday afternoon I thought about it just as I dozed off for a nap. I figured I'd bake them next weekend. No, that's when I leave for Phoenix—

Sound familiar? It's called being long on talk but short on follow through. Caring dads minimize such instances.

Selfishness. It might be tough, but I thought it worth a try. I called Toni with the news. "Listen, I'm really sorry, but I have an emergency. Can we reschedule the marriage counseling appointment? How's tomorrow evening look?"

She couldn't make it then, and I was committed to other things the following day. So she settled for the next Monday night—if she could coax her husband into coming.

Everybody knows that emergencies come up. Sometimes a change of plans can't be helped. But what was my sudden diversion? My neighbor came home about 3:00 P.M. to tell me, "I've got Laker playoff tickets for tonight. Can you go?"

I'd been working hard. I needed a break. And nobody, I mean nobody, plays more exciting ball than the Lakers. I decided to reward myself.

But I broke my word. I felt guilty the whole evening. Besides that, the Lakers lost.

There's nothing wrong with having some fun and setting aside time for it. The problem comes when we circumvent prior commitments to achieve it.

Unmeasurable promises. Most families complain that dads don't communicate enough. Lots of dads prefer to be observers rather than full participants in family life. But, when we do talk, sometimes we don't think through the implications of what we say.

Suppose you're driving down the road and see a huge brightly-painted billboard advertising a gigantic amusement park in a neighboring city. Little Tommy cries from the back seat, "Daddy! Daddy! I want to go to the Hills of Thrills!"

To which you reply, "Well, yes, I suppose we ought to go there someday."

Nice statement: "ought to—someday." There's absolutely no promise intended here. That way, if you never get around to going, you can still be a man of your word, right?

But what did little Tommy hear? Tommy tells the neighbor kids, "My dad said he was going to take us to the Hills of Thrills!"

If it's the kind of place you envision taking the family, make it definite. Set a date on the calendar even if it's months away. If the kids are too small to go now, tell them, "As soon as you are eight, we'll go to the Hills of Thrills."

If, on the other hand, the adventure's too dangerous, too far to travel, or too expensive, tell Tommy the truth.

Caring dads work to make promises measurable.

Lack of enthusiasm. It wasn't a promise. Jan and I were just visiting, and we tossed around the idea that maybe we'd go out to the steak house for dinner.

Later Dave stopped by the office and invited me out to lunch. There's nothing worse than eating two meals out in the same day. After the luncheon date I felt like I was coming down with a cold or something. I was exhausted even before I started my evening five-mile run. After the run I hoped Jan had forgotten about any dinner plans. Besides, we hadn't really said for sure—had we?

As I huffed and puffed into the house, I found Jan fixing her hair and slipping on some jewelry. *Uh oh,* I thought, *please, not tonight. I need a peaceful evening at home. Just a little rest—*

Fortunately, I didn't say that out loud. Instead, I showered, cleaned up, and went to the steak house. I sure didn't feel like going. But being a man of my word doesn't depend upon my feelings. It depends on my decision to make my words valid.

Expediency. We're all in a hurry to get somewhere. We race through the week to get to the weekend. Then the weekend's a hectic mess. We work hard all year looking forward to vacation. We get so worn out on vacation we can hardly wait to get home. Every meal's a rush because there are meetings to attend, TV shows to watch, projects to complete. Too many folk in our day spend entire lifetimes racing to the future, never enjoying the present.

For some, the making or breaking of promises propels us past today to the grand future of achievement. We only volunteer to paint the big sign for the service club barbecue when we think we're going to be nominated for first vice president. Sure we said we'd pick up those concert tickets, but waiting that long in line means hitting the rush-hour traffic on the freeway.

Keeping promises fluctuates with their value to a private agenda or convenience.

Just how important is keeping your word, anyway? If I did decide it was important, what could I do to improve my integrity in this area? Here are some suggestions.

First, consider your influence. A trustworthy man impacts his entire world. However, he won't be assured of material success. In our morally off-kilter world, many times the deceitful appear to prosper. But the man of integrity is remembered and respected. The man who follows through on every hint of a promise, the one who lets you know where he stands, stands tall. You may not agree with him, but when all is said and done, you respect him.

Small promises kept build blocks of trust for bigger ones. Sometime in the past you made a whopper of a promise to your wife. It went something like this: "I do promise before God and these witnesses to be thy loving and faithful husband."

How does your wife know you're keeping this promise? Because you're a man who keeps all other promises: the promise to be home by 6:00 P.M. or to sit down and write to your mom or to take Tommy to soccer practice.

As a Christian, I look forward to Christ's return. The Bible clearly states in such places as Acts 1:11 and Matthew 16:27-28 that He will. Yet, it's been a long time since He was here on earth. So how do I know He's really coming back? Because He's kept every other promise. He's a man of His word. I've no reason to doubt the promises I haven't seen completed yet.

Little promises, whether made by men or God, prove the validity of the big ones.

We must also remember that our example teaches another generation. We influence our own family. Exhorting a child to keep promises gives him the right idea. Living a model life of integrity gives him a standard to follow. We've no right to demand more faithfulness from our children's mouths than they can see in ours.

Second, ask for your family's help. The biggest weakness man has is not admitting he has a weakness. If you decide you want to be a man of your word, tell your family. Gather them around the table and say, "Listen, gang, I'm going to try to do everything I promise you I'll do, but I need your help. I get so busy, so tired, so hassled sometimes, that it's hard to follow through. I won't think you're nagging me if you remind me of what I'm supposed to do."

To help make promises measurable, encourage them to plan dates with you. Buy an extra-large calendar, and write down specific dates.

It might fit your family to obtain a bulletin board with just your name on it. If any family member needs to remind you of something, he can stick a note to this board. In fact, it wouldn't hurt for every family member to have such a bulletin board.

Third, seek the Lord's help. To think you can change your life totally through your own initiative is foolish. If you could change your life so easily, it would have been changed by now. Some changes are tough. You have to blast your way through ingrained habits. To admit to God and to others that you need help is the first step to proving you're serious.

What can God do for you?

He can give you wisdom: "But if any of you lacks wisdom, let him ask of God, who gives to all men generously and without reproach, and it will be given to him" (James 1:5).

He can straighten priorities: "But seek first His kingdom and His righteousness; and all these things shall be added to you" (Matthew 6:33).

He can prompt right actions: "But the Helper, the Holy Spirit, whom the Father will send in My name, He will teach you all things, and bring to your remembrance all that I said to you" (John 14:26).

I suppose there's a possibility that a man could get so tied up with saying the right things, he'd hardly say anything at all. But there's no need for that extreme. Words are the glue for relationships. Serious communication as well as the lighthearted fun helps to build the strength of intimacy among people.

Some of the wildest stories ever told were probably those uttered around the lonely campfires of cowboys driving huge herds north. These men often survived months without seeing anyone else outside their immediate outfit. The trail provided little to read. Sparse news reached them from the civilized world. Their main entertainment consisted of "yarnin'."

Sitting around the campfire, they made up grand stories of daring exploits and hilarious encounters. These oral short stories were perfected and memorized during the long hours in the saddle.

However, when a man said, "Now, speaking for the ranch,—" all the others knew that the statement following would not be a made-up story. It would be the truth. When someone spoke for "the ranch" there could be no exaggeration. Too much money and too many lives depended on it.

Our own family, friends, and business acquaintances need to un-

derstand when we're "speaking for the ranch." We can joke and
laugh and kid and play, but when it comes time to promise, our word
stands.

King Solomon dedicated the magnificent new Temple in Jerusalem with prayer. He praised God by reviewing His faithfulness in all
that He had spoken. "Blessed be the Lord, who has given rest to His
people Israel, according to all that He promised; not one word has
failed of all His good promise, which He promised through Moses
His servant" (1 Kings 8:56).

Not one word failed! That's what you call integrity. That's our
prime example to follow. But it doesn't come by merely wishing for
it. It happens when we decide to work on just one area at a time. It
starts when we put down this book and go fulfill one nagging promise
that hangs over our heads.

The result won't be instant perfection, but it might be a notice-
able improvement.

5

Caring Dads Treat the Family Like the Preacher's There

I sat in the barber shop waiting for a haircut. The other men spouted stories that got wilder and wilder. Finally, after a particularly profane outburst, the barber turned to me and said, "Well, Reverend, what do you think of that?"

Suddenly, the speaker hemmed and hawed, then blurted out, "Oh, sorry about that. I didn't know we had a preacher in the crowd."

There are some folks who by instinct try to clean up their act around spiritual people.

How about you?

Your wife invites the pastor over for dinner after church. Your only worry is your five-year-old son, Harold. He's been obnoxious the past few weeks, and it's been quite a struggle to keep him in line. So for several days prior to the pastor's visit, you coach Harold on proper etiquette. At least his table manners will be in line.

On the day of the big event, Harold begins by kicking the preacher's shin, dumping a box of blocks on his wife's lap, and knocking over the potted plant. During the fancy meal, which includes the best linen tablecloth, crystal glasses, and china, you seat little Harold as far away from the pastor and his wife as possible. Yet he won't sit still. You give him several subtle jabs, hoping he'll settle down. Then it happens.

Harold elbows his milk glass, and the contents catapult past the pot roast along the seam of the linen. Milk oozes between the cracks in the table, dripping on the preacher's pant leg.

Your first reaction is to grab little Harold, march him off to his room, and place some appropriate discomfort to his backside. Such a desire is stifled by the thought of present company. You say, instead, something like, "Now, don't worry about it, Harold. Daddy will help clean up the mess." But let little Harold try the same thing tomorrow, when that important person isn't there, and the story is often quite different.

Should it be?

Why don't we practice holiness at home?

What impresses our families most is what I call "Home Holiness." We can't expect our kids to behave better than they see us acting in the privacy of our homes. Here are some suggestions for building a spiritual home.

First, be genuine. Make sure each family member knows how you became a person of faith in Christ. This is no time for charades. Some may pretend there's a Santa Claus for several years with the tiny ones because it's a once-a-year event, and it doesn't demand too much. But when we discuss spiritual matters, that's another story. We're talking about eternity. We're talking about a choice between life and death.

If you're not sure what you believe, find out in a hurry. I was twenty-three before I was ready to admit that I needed God. Even though I had a wife, family, job, and home that I enjoyed, life stretched ahead like one long rut.

Before long I found a small home Bible study where I learned how a man must accept Jesus Christ as Savior and Lord. So I did.

That was in 1967, but I remember it well. How come? Because I often relate the story to others. I've told it so often that my son once said, "Do we have to listen to that again? I know it all by heart!"

We can't guarantee the spiritual choices of our children. God still gives them the freedom to make their own decisions. But we can provide fertile environments for their own discovery of the Lord God. They need to learn early how spiritual life begins and how, in particular, yours began.

Second, let them see you in study and prayer.

I'm well aware of the warning in Matthew 6:6, "But you, when you pray, go into your inner room."

All of us, even in the most hectic of households, need private times of prayer. Yet not everything is to be done in hiding.

Daniel understood the significance of King Darius's decree forbidding prayer. Yet the Scriptures say, "Now when Daniel knew that the document was signed, he entered his house (now in his roof chamber he had windows open toward Jerusalem); and he continued kneeling on his knees three times a day, praying and giving thanks before his God, as he had been doing previously" (Daniel 6:10).

After Paul had a short ministry in the city of Tyre, the Scriptures relate: "And when it came about that our days there were ended, we departed and started on our journey, while they all, with wives and children, escorted us until we were out of the city. And after kneeling down on the beach and praying, we said farewell to one another" (Acts 21:5).

We teach our family to pray by their listening to us. So we pray as we tuck the little ones in bed. We pause to offer thanks before meals. We pray when we hurt. And we pray when we rejoice. Through these exercises we teach our children the form and language of prayer. Yet we need to do more—we need to demonstrate the importance of personal prayer.

When you tell Junior that Daddy can't play with him until he's finished his prayer time, you make a powerful statement to a young, impressionable mind. When Junior sees this pattern year after year, the message sinks in: "Daddy really believes in prayer."

We shouldn't overwhelm our children with constant, pious displays of spirituality. But they should see a natural overflow from our inward spiritual life.

When Aaron rises early, he'll often find Mom and Dad in the office, studying the Bible and praying. When that happens he knows he'll have to wait before making any loud requests. When he must have something, he softly knocks at the door. At age five, he doesn't know a lot about prayer and the Bible. But he does know they're important to his parents.

Caring dads teach spiritual discipline by example.

Third, make conversation natural. The deepest spiritual lessons aren't always learned at a family devotional time but rather during the busy pace of living. When the kids know the lecture is coming, they'll often take it for just that—a sermon to be endured. They learn best when the truth of God jumps out from an ordinary activity.

Russell, at seven, enjoyed going to work with me. Work, at that time, meant physical labor on the family farm. One spring day we loaded young orange trees from our nursery for a buyer's fields. As I swung trees on the truck, Russ and I bantered about many things. As we laughed I retorted, "Straighten up or I'll send you back where you came from."

He quipped, "Oh, you mean back to Mommy's tummy?"

That touched off to me the account of Nicodemus visiting Jesus. So, I related the story to Russell: "And then Jesus told him he had to be born again. When Nicodemus protested that a person couldn't go back into his mother's womb, Jesus explained that it meant a spiritual birth."

The conversation kept it's fast, lighthearted pace until I noticed Russell's thoughtful expression. "You know, Dad," he finally said, "I've never been born again."

"Would you like to be?" I asked.

"Yeah."

After a few minutes spent explaining what that meant, I knelt down with Russ in the dirt behind the old broken-down barn, next to some rusty, antiquated farm machinery. There he asked Jesus into his life.

Caring dads watch for ways to instigate spiritual conversations.

How can you shape up your Home Holiness? Here's a checklist.

Rate your Bible study. Would you call your practice strong? OK?

Weak? Set yourself a reasonable goal. If you're not involved in a study plan already, how about a system that gets you through the whole Bible in a year? Every December, tract societies and Christian bookstores offer guides to show you a daily schedule for doing that. Another plan might be to read two Old Testament chapters and two New Testament chapters every day.

Let your family know what you're up to. Encourage them to adopt a similar goal. Also, ask them to help you keep yours up. Make "Daddy, did you read your Bible chapters?" an acceptable statement any day.

Keep a note pad handy as you read. Jot down one spiritual truth that's worth sharing with someone else. Take the time to tell someone about what you're reading.

Rate your prayer life. Is it strong? OK? Weak? One important aspect of praying is consistency. Plug away day after day, week after week, year after year, striving for meaningful conversations with God.

Our wall phone hangs right next to our breakfast counter, which means I often end up talking on the phone during a family meal. It doesn't surprise my family anymore when I stop a conversation to pray with a caller on the phone—another way prayer is made a natural part of everyday life.

If you really want to prove the importance of prayer to your family, let them see you give up something important to keep your appointed prayer time. They won't soon forget your priority if you flip off your favorite televised sporting event to have that time alone in prayer.

Rate your reflection time. Do you spend time reflecting on spiritual truth often? Occasionally? Seldom?

Sunday lunch time can be an opportunity to have each child tell one thing they learned at Sunday school that morning. The older ones and adults could relate one thing from the sermon they'd like to make a part of their life. Keep asking, "What does God want me to do with this information?"

Select a Christian television or radio program to listen to as a family each week. You might keep a family journal of the questions and answers generated each session.

Ask your family their opinion concerning a passage you're studying or a problem you're trying to solve. Listen to what they have to say. Sometimes kids say just the thing we need to hear.

Rate your success or failure honestly. Do you allow your family to share in your successes and your failures often? Occasionally? Seldom? Your family needs to know how God provides for you, guides you, and empowers you. They should witness God's wisdom benefiting your everyday concerns. They should hear about God's answer to your prayers. This builds a healthy expectancy within them that God is willing to act.

It's just as crucial to be honest about struggles too. Sometimes we don't know all the answers. At times we fail. If all we allow our family to glimpse is an image of perfection, their own imperfection may depress them.

Several years ago my wife and I sat around good-naturedly reviewing our flops. There were times when we had organized programs and no one showed up, people we had tried to help spiritually who left the church instead, great works attempted for God that failed. On and on it went. Our son Mike asked, "Did they really all happen to you?"

For eighteen years he'd only heard about the successes. Once he knew that we'd tried many things that didn't work, he felt freer to go for some things on his own. Up to that point he'd felt a little intimidated, thinking everything he did had to be a roaring victory.

Rate your openness to God's changes. Are you open to God's direction? Somewhat interested? Closed? How about asking your family to make some suggestions about how you could be different. Ask them, "If you could get the Lord to change one area in my life, what would you ask Him to change?"

Now understand that many family members would hesitate to answer such a question with honesty. You might want to help them out. Put the question on a blackboard where everyone can see it. Allow them to anonymously place their answers underneath. They can do this over several days time. Then, surprise them by working to change, as the Lord confirms them to you, the areas that need work.

What are you doing in all this? Practicing holiness. Just like a ball player practices the basic fundamentals of the game, so we Christian dads must practice over and over the basics of our walk of faith. First John 3:7 is specific: "Little children, let no one deceive you; the one who practices righteousness is righteous, just as He is righteous."

Rate your spiritual adventure level. Are you willing to take risks for the pursuit of spiritual advancements? Would you say you're adventurous? Cautious? Stuck in a rut?

The great thing about being in God's family is that we're all His children. Whether we're three, thirteen, thirty, or sixty, when we've trusted Him we're children of God. And it's all right to act like children sometimes. We can explore new things because we're still trying to find out who we are.

Whether you organize a home Bible study, a backyard kids club, or a living Christmas card for your neighbors, demonstrate the fact that following Christ provides excitement, adventure, and challenge. Show others that it's acceptable to risk something big for God.

I find that most dads find it easier to do all the right things out in public rather than at home. There are some good reasons for that. Let's look at some of the ememics of "Home Holiness."

Emergencies. The best-laid plans of men—usually only get half done. Whether it's building a new shelf for the garage or diving into a personal Bible study program, emergencies ruin our schedules.

It's always on the day that you get up extra early to study that you find the hot water heater leaking. It's the afternoon that you determine not to yell at Junior that he spray paints his bike—in his room. It's always during your prayer time that Missy falls off her swing. When you're in the middle of a good discussion with your wife, the phone always rings.

Most of us view emergencies as adequate causes for ceasing whatever project we're involved in. Once diverted, we often don't get back to it.

Two years ago I resolved to lose weight by jogging everyday. I made up my mind not to let anything divert me from that plan. I now run about twelve miles a day. Only once in two years did I stop short of my predetermined goal.

I can't count how many days I awoke tired, hurting, bored, unmotivated, or all of the above. Yet I forced myself to keep going. In rain, snow, fog, high winds, and intense heat, I've continued to run. In spite of blisters, side splints, colds, pulled muscles, cramps, and migraines, I ran.

You've done the same thing—in your own areas of interest. If something is important enough, nothing can keep you back. We must develop that same attitude toward our spiritual discipline. Nothing should prevent our obedience to Christ's leading in our home life.

Well, almost nothing.

Recently, for the first time, I had a run interrupted. A young man prepared to make a mad dash across a busy Phoenix intersection during the morning rush-hour traffic. He stepped in front of a speeding car just as I jogged by. I stopped to shield the wounded man from traffic until some paramedics arrived. Then they whizzed him off to the hospital. I stuck around to answer questions for the police. Now that was an emergency. I had to stop.

We have real emergencies that can halt our spiritual disciplines. Missy's bleeding elbow does need care. However, we need to handle the emergency and return to what was interrupted as quickly as possible. After the police interrogated me, I completed my morning rounds.

Desire. We can be honest. Sometimes we don't want to do what's right. Sure, I know I should relax and forget the fact that Junior bent my five iron. But I don't always want to relax. And I don't want to spend twenty minutes on my knees in prayer. There are times I don't want to spend even two minutes. I don't want to get up early to read—I don't want to get up at all.

So what's new?

Sometimes we don't feel like going to work. But we do. Other times we know we'd definitely rather not visit the in-laws, but we do.

There are times we don't want to stop by the store and bring home some milk and bread, but we drive the three miles out of the way.

We allow duty to surpass desire in order to accomplish quality in our family relationships. But we shouldn't downplay duty as a motive. Duty has propelled civilization on a steadier course than desire for centuries.

Lack of strength. Tiredness tends to weaken our concern for holiness at home. Many times I put in eighty-hour weeks. By the time I get home, what I want more than anything is rest, peace, and quiet. I don't want to open my eyes to read. I don't want to concentrate on anything serious. I don't want to hear my wife's problems. I don't want to hear the new song my five-year-old learned. And I certainly don't want someone to drop by the house for a visit.

Of course, not every night leaves me feeling like that. But some do. Yet, even in that condition, I still do some things.

How many meals would Mom have cooked for me when I was a kid if she never cooked when she was tired? Where would our freedoms be today if the generals let anyone go home who got tired while fighting our wars? And where would God's salvation be if Jesus Christ quit because the cross-examinations, beatings, and lack of sleep made Him want to quit?

Lack of strength isn't a valid excuse for slacking off in holiness at home.

Ignorance. Lack of knowledge kills spiritual vitality in the home. It's possible for a man to avoid considering the spiritual obligations of family living. Yet a commitment to Christ means obedience to His words: "The one who says he abides in Him ought himself to walk in the same manner as He walked" (1 John 2:6).

I just received my annual shock: the property tax bill. This year I was sure there was a mistake, so I read all the fine print on the back of the statement. It didn't tell me how to lower my bill, but it did say that I owed the money on the prescribed date whether I received this tax notice or not.

Total ignorance of property tax laws doesn't exempt me from paying the assessment. The same is true with God's Word. You might not know it. You can ignore it. But you're still responsible to obey it.

Lack of accountability. We might have kids that fuss and a wife that nags, but in reality there's no one around who can make us shape up. And we do need help. A very wise man will listen to his family and spiritual peers and allow the Holy Spirit to use them to prompt better family living.

Most of the successful dads I know get involved with local church fellowships. They commit themselves to Bible study groups where they talk about struggles with discipline. Caring dads find a way to build in their own accountability.

Craig and I have been friends for a long time. He's a guy who always keeps an even temper. He seems to always know the right words to say and makes others feel comfortable in his presence. In fact, he's so consistent that I unconsciously began looking for a flaw. *Sure, he's Mister Nice Guy in public. But what's he like at home?* I thought.

One night I did see him at home. His wife, Carol, was preparing to serve dessert, so I walked into the kitchen and drilled her. "What's Craig really like? Does he ever blow his top? Is he a bear to live with?"

"He's not the same at home as he is in public," she said.

"I knew it!" I began.

Her eyes twinkled. "He saves the best part of himself for home."

That's the way a caring dad operates.

6

Caring Dads Keep the Office Door Open

Buzzers annoy me.

Beepers drive me crazy.

Watches that signal the hour give me a pain.

But my biggest nightmare is the thought that some day I'll have to install a car phone and surrender my last bastion of privacy.

I do love people. It's fulfilling to me to work at a job that deals with meeting people's needs. Yet there are times I need space. Quiet, empty space.

When I'm working on a sermon, writing a book or article, or counseling someone with a serious family problem, I often tell my secretary to hold all the calls and keep all visitors from my door. The one exception to that strict rule: Janet, the boys, and my mother. They are to be put through no matter what. I don't ever want to get so busy that I can't take time to talk to my family.

Recently I interviewed a young man for a staff position at our church. At the key point in a discussion about leadership styles and philosophies of ministry, I told my secretary to hold the calls. Fifteen minutes into the interview, the phone buzzer rang. Susan announced that my son, Mike, was on line one.

The flow of the interview was interrupted as I took the call. Mike asked me for a few dollars for gas for his Jeep. We just got back to the job discussion when there was a knock at the office door. Mike

stepped in to get the money. Once again, we had to stop, then re-
engage the conversation.

Some might say this was a wasted distraction. I see it differently.

I believe I made two important statements by allowing Mike to interrupt. First, I reinforced the idea to Mike that he's important.
When he wants to talk, Dad's ready to listen. Bumming four bucks
for gasoline may be a small deal, but it helps establish the line of
communication. When the big crisis comes, Mike knows Dad's
available.

Second, the man sitting in the office, who thought he wanted to
spend some years ministering to our youth, could see that one dad
considered his kids important. A pastor can preach every Sunday
about how to treat a family, but it's his relationship with his own
family that's most convincing.

Jesus said, "Let the children alone, and do not hinder them from
coming to Me, for the kingdom of heaven belongs to such as these"
(Matthew 19:14). From this passage and the parallel accounts in
Mark 10:13-16 and Luke 18:15-17, it's possible to reconstruct the
following scene.

After Jesus dialogued with the religious leaders of the day, He began to teach a great crowd of people. In their midst, some Pharisees
disputed His authority and teaching. The legalistic teachings of the
Pharisees strayed from the intent of the Old Testament. Jesus cor-
rected their error about an important and emotional issue: divorce.
The climate tensed; the crowd strained to catch each word.

Meanwhile, some parents pushed their way forward, shoving their
little Jacobs and Rebekahs toward Jesus with hopes that He would
touch and bless them. They seemed oblivious to the depth of the issues swirling around them.

The apostles, acting as bodyguards and shields for the Master,
tried to chase the kids away. "Don't bother Jesus with trivia," they
implied, "He's too busy to hold and kiss babies."

But Jesus let them come. He never lost sight of the truly important
things of life. We need His example to remind us to do the same.

Intrusions come not only at work but during leisure too. After a
tiring day of racing from one crisis to another, I flopped in my easy
chair, grabbed up the newspaper, and flipped on the TV to watch a

football game. I had about an hour and a half before I needed to return to the church for a meeting.

I had just buried myself in the newspaper when Aaron flew into the house screaming, "Daddy's home! Daddy's home!" He leaped into my lap, shoved the paper aside, grabbed my face so that I had to look him in the eye, and said, "Hi, buddy! Want to play?"

I didn't. But I couldn't remember the last time I'd taken time to play with him. So down went the paper, and off went the set. Out came the stack of children's books, and for the 937th time we laughed our way through Go, Dog, Go.

Aaron's too young to realize how tiring a job can be. He doesn't even comprehend what kinds of things a pastor has to do. But he does understand that when a dad loves his son he is willing to read books to him.

Later I grabbed a bite to eat and headed out the door to my meeting. "Bye, Daddy," he called. "I love you very, very much."

I felt greatly refreshed.

Caring dads work at being accessible to their families.

Before we succumb to indignation over the interruptions our children make for us, we'd do well to consider these four questions.

First, is this a reasonable demand for a person of this age and maturity?

Suppose you're halfway through pruning the overgrown juniper in the front yard when four-year-old Joey tears across the flower bed yelling, "Daddy, can we play ball?"

Whether or not you stop is your decision, but for a little guy his age the fact that you're busy doesn't faze him. His world centers around play, and Daddy happens to be his favorite playmate. So there's Dad, outside, there's Joey, outside—and ball is played outside.

To turn and bark, "Can't you see I'm pruning?" fails to address the context of the question.

A better response would be, "Joey, I love playing ball. But this old plant has gotten so big we can't see out our window. I'm almost through cutting it, so I'd better finish. It would sure look funny if I left it half cut, wouldn't it? Besides, if I cut it good it'll be easier to find the baseballs that fly over here. We might even find an old base-ball in there now. Why don't you help me put the trimmings in the trash can?"

If the demand's unreasonable, we should take the time to point out why. We don't hurry out of the shower to help Junior pick up his blocks. We don't cancel tomorrow's business lunch because it's Missy's Cabbage Patch doll's birthday. We don't turn off the World Series so Butch can watch cartoon reruns. Even some reasonable re-quests might have to be rejected, but we still need to take time to see the situation from the child's viewpoint.

Second, what will the outcome be if I ignore this interruption?

After all, people are what life and family are all about. Civilization doesn't survive because of schedules or programs but because of peo-ple. Great discoveries aren't made by machines but by people. God didn't send His Son into the world so that we could complete our things-to-do lists but rather to save sinful people like you, me, and those around us.

Ask yourself, Can I gracefully postpone this intrusion without any serious damage to a relationship or anyone's Christian commitment?

Suppose I am talking to Mrs. Hunter on the phone about her son who was recently hospitalized for an unknown disease. Suddenly, Aaron comes screaming through the house. "Daddy, do you want to hear me count to one hundred in Spanish?" To postpone the count-ing marathon would cause less strain in relationships than to show disinterest in the hurts of the Hunter family.

Third, why do I resent this interruption? Is it fatigue? Is it lack of interest in the person or subject?

Junior asks you to take him to the city park and then to a fast-food joint for lunch. A playground full of noisy kids and a plate of half-cooked chicken don't stir your imagination. But some people are worth overriding your personal comfort.

Fourth, can I suggest a better alternative?

We don't have to be maneuvered by every demand on our time.

Some must be declined. But we can still try to suggest alternatives that show we care.

Missy wants you to take her shopping this afternoon to pick out a racket for the tennis team. You tell her that since Friday's your day off, that would be a better day for you. Then the two of you could have time to travel to the sports center.

It's possible to be dedicated to a job and your family at the same time—without your family's resenting the time you have to take for working. Here are some suggestions for improving the quality of your time together.

Give them all your attention. When it's time to play blocks with Junior, don't try to watch TV, talk to your wife, and eat dinner at the same time. Demonstrate your devotion by throwing yourself into one project at a time.

One suggestion is to instigate "Daddy Days." Set aside a day when you and one of the kids can do whatever he decides. If you have some budget or other restrictions, let him know ahead of time. But let him plan the day. You could find yourself playing with a Barbie doll for three hours or chasing balls through a miniature golf course. But that's the chance you take.

On a recent Daddy Day at our house, Aaron led me through five different playgrounds, followed by lunch at McDonald's. The price of the day, minus gas, totaled $4.87. I've found that one good Daddy Day can help a little one forget a month of nights when I'm called away to meetings.

Never use money as a Daddy substitute. I've never met a child yet that felt alienated from Dad because he refused to buy him something he begged for. But there are many who think of Dad as a stranger because he never spends any time with them.

Whenever I travel and speak, I try to bring a little present to Aaron. But I put a restriction on the gift. I must be willing on my return to play with him and the new toy. The toy doesn't buy off my days of being away; it's a tool to reunite us as father and son.

Take them to work with you. Let them know what you do with your days away from home. To get an idea of what you might need to clear up in their minds, ask your children ahead of time what it is they think you do.

Show them where you park the car, where you do your work, the product you make, the problems you must solve. Show them where you eat your lunch. Find a way to allow each child to view the inside operations.

Once I showed Aaron how the phone system works in my office and how the buzzer catches my attention. That way he could visualize what's going on when he calls me on the phone.

I've taken him with me on hospital visits (though he has to wait in the lobby) to let him know that some people are hurting and Dad needs to visit them sometimes. I've let him go up to the front of the sanctuary after a service and stand in the pulpit like he was the preacher. Whenever I travel to speak, I pull out a map and show him where I'm going. Then I mark the calendar with the dates I will leave and return.

Teach them one of your skills. A neighbor boy visited our home, and he happened to tell me he knew how to read a transit. Then he explained how to set it up level, how to focus it, and how to tell which post is higher than the other. His dad is a surveyor.

If you can, teach your children how to saw straight and pound nails. Teach them how to use a calculator or computer, or how to type, or how to sell watches. You'll not only help them find their own fields of interest and expertise, but you'll have something in common with each other.

Learn a new skill together. How about finding a class that each of you can enroll in? Deliberately pick a subject where you begin on the same level as they do. You'll probably excel faster, but it's good for them to see that you don't know everything, that everyone has to begin somewhere. Allow your children to watch you learn something new.

Watch their favorite TV program with them. You may have no idea what your children watch. But you may hear bits and pieces about things like a bionic pickup that turns into a giant man and saves the universe. Sit down with them when you get a chance and watch a whole show. Allow them to explain what's going on so you can see it the way they're seeing it.

Caring dads, for the most part, let the family interrupt their activities, and they work at finding quality time together.

But caring dads realize that moms need attention as well. Here are a few ideas for helping to build strength in a marriage relationship when daily hassles and pressures foster irritations.

Give her a daily survey of activities. You don't have to take more than ten minutes, but try to run through your day. Cover the projects you worked on, the significant conversations you had, the ideas that popped into your mind, the ups and the downs. Try to tie her into your world at the points where she's interested, so she doesn't feel as though she only knows half of you.

Help her escape her confines. Whether she stays at home or works, she could feel as though she's in a rut. Help her get into that painting or writing class. Listen to her dreams. Think of ways you can help her fulfill them. Maybe you can accomplish them together.

Build her up at work. Talk about your spouse's positive traits with those on the job. Sooner or later the word will get back to her, and a compliment from you received through others can mean a lot. Let others know that you're married to one neat, mature, talented gal who adds so much to your life that without her you couldn't achieve half of what you do.

Consult her. Many women enjoy assessing people and situations. If this is true of your wife, use her expertise to help you understand the people you work with. If she knows your colleagues, get her opinion of their moods and needs. If she can't meet them, tell her some of the interaction struggles. See what she thinks about it.

Give her good listening time. Don't just hurry home and unload your day's hassles without giving her a chance to do the same. Look her in the eyes and really listen. You hurry home after a six-day trip with your head stuffed full of great events to share. But don't assume her world stood still until you returned.

Apply her areas of expertise. If you're swamped and she's a good reader, see if she'd like to scan that book you've needed to study, marking the best parts. If she has a flare for interior decorating, ask her for suggestions for your office. If she spent years working in a bank, have her peer at the fine print on a business loan.

I'm sitting here with forty resumés on my desk from people applying for a staff position with us. Jan loves to read about other people's lives, so she's happy to comb through the pile for me and leave her comments and reactions attached to each one.

Ask for her prayer support. Caring dads know that a good family and vocational career flow out of spiritual resources. The two of you can agree together in prayer about many things: the children, the church, the needs of friends. Why not include the hassles and pressures of the job, too? Asking your wife to pray for something about the job tells her two important things: one, you admit you're not self-sufficient and you do need God's help; and two, you imply that you recognize her spiritual equality.

I'm not sure it's entirely true, but it seems that things were simpler in the past. Dad's work meant going out to the family farm to feed the animals, plant the crops, and hoe the weeds. Mom and the kids might help with the chores. There was little separation between job and home. Certainly that's not true now. Too many family members live in divergent worlds. There's Mom's work. There's Dad's work. There's the kids' school. At best, everyone gets together for a meal or two. Dads who are willing to work at it can reverse this trend.

Just how important are our kids? If we listed those things that count more than they do, what would be on the list? A car? A house? A job? A sport? A hobby? Think it through carefully in your own life.

However, to say our kids are more important than, say, our car, doesn't mean we would encourage them to drive it anytime, anywhere, and wreck it. But it could mean we'd sell it in a minute to send them to college. It could mean our first concern if they were in an accident would be their safety, not the car's condition.

If we say they're more important than our jobs, it might mean refusing to make a business appointment the night of the class play. It might mean turning down a promotion during a child's senior year because a move would be devastating. It might mean passing up some overtime instead of canceling the family vacation.

Your family is important. So why not let them know how important they are? Caring dads let the kids bust through the office door.

7

Caring Dads Let Them Go

A couple years ago I wanted my wife to have some time to herself. So on Friday, my day off, I said, "Honey, I'll take care of Aaron today. Why don't you take some money, the car, and just go anywhere you want and do anything you want? Go shopping. Or go to the beach. Or go visit a friend."

She looked at me as though to say, "You're kidding!" but she answered, "I will!"

And she did.

While Aaron and I played in every kiddie park in a twenty-mile radius, Janet headed to a mountain lake. She found a comfy spot under a tree, pulled out a novel she'd wanted to read for years, and enjoyed six hours of carefree bliss. No telephone. No child whining. No clutter staring her in the face. Just sunshine, blue skies, sparkling water, and an occasional sailboat.

She even took a short nap, then drove down to a neighboring town for a late lunch. She told me later, "You know, that's the first time in my life I ever entered a restaurant alone. It was a whole new experience."

We'd been married twenty years, but her need for a little privacy had never dawned on me before.

Caring dads make sure every family member has some private time to himself.

Jesus said to His disciples, "Come away by yourselves to a lonely place and rest a while" (Mark 6:31).

Earlier in that same chapter, Mark says that Jesus sent the disciples out on their own, two by two, into the cities and villages. They preached the news about Christ and ministered to people's hurts and oppression. When they regrouped they shared their experiences. As always, a big crowd began to form around Jesus. Jesus knew they needed some time away from the crowds. It was a principle He often followed: "And in the early morning, while it was still dark, He arose and went out and departed to a lonely place, and was praying there" (Mark 1:35). "And after bidding them farewell, He departed to the mountain to pray" (Mark 6:46).

At another time, right before the important job of selecting the twelve apostles, "it was at this time that He went off to the mountain to pray, and He spent the whole night in prayer to God" (Luke 6:12).

Everyone needs privacy. I believe there are special groups within our society who desperately need times alone. Caring dads can help insure that they get it.

Mothers of preschoolers. No other group has every waking moment so thoroughly planned by others as do the mothers of preschoolers. I've visited prisoners in state penitentiaries who had more privacy than a mom with a three-year-old and six-month-old.

Adding a child to the family doubles the physical and mental workload. Care of a small child equals two forty-hour jobs in one week. Care of two small children can be like three forty-hour jobs. I'm amazed at the physical, mental, and spiritual stamina it requires. Someone needs to give mothers some time off.

People facing major decisions. Anyone in your family thinking about a change in jobs, getting married, or moving needs some think time. Minds need opportunity to chart out pros and cons, consider alternatives, dream and imagine all the consequences and potential. Such disciplines suffer when trapped in the obligations of a hectic family atmosphere.

Kids from large families. Any child who has to cope with cramped living quarters needs a privacy outlet. When three or four brothers share the same bedroom, it's next to impossible to discover a separate identity. What a child thinks, believes, and really wants to do becomes blurred with the family personality.

People with crisis-centered jobs. Part of the agony and glory of being a pastor is the day-after-day, year-after-year responsibility of dealing with broken marriages, runaway kids, grieving parents, hurting teens, bitter neighbors, and angry dads.

But pastors aren't the only ones who need time alone. So do professional counselors, teachers, lawyers, doctors, social workers, bank clerks, and waitresses. If your job throws you constantly into intense situations, you need to get away alone.

All teens. Did you ever stop to consider how many life-changing decisions are made between the ages of thirteen and twenty? Kids today deal with sex, marriage, alcohol and drugs, college, jobs, self-identity, and spiritual destiny. Good decisions don't always evolve from the peer pressure of friends or the nagging of family.

Here are some biblical examples of reasons we need to sometimes be alone:

For rest. Mark 3:20 says that Jesus "came home, and the multitude gathered again, to such an extent that they could not even eat a meal."

No one has accused me, yet, of being lazy. I'm up before five, run twelve miles a day, and fly through a heavy workload. But I work at getting rest too. If at all possible, I'm in bed by nine. And I take advantage of my vacation time to get away for relaxation.

For hiding. In 1 Kings 19:1-4, Elijah fled to the wilderness. He had accomplished a great work for God. The prophets of Baal had been destroyed on Mount Carmel. But now he was afraid for his life. He needed a place to hide.

In a desert cave he finally caught his breath. Here, God told him to get back into the thick of things. His work wasn't done. Elijah needed that time alone to hear the voice of God. In the sound "of a gentle blowing" God revealed Himself—not the kind of sound you can distinguish in the noisy throng.

God doesn't let us stay in hiding for long. He scooted Elijah out of his cave after a short while, but the time he spent there had value. To find a cave we might have to unplug the phone, lock the door, and then rest in His quiet peace.

For prayer. Did you notice that in all the passages mentioned above, Jesus desired private time in order to pray?

Public prayer is important. Together, we join our hearts and voices to bring God praise, to seek His wisdom, and to overcome the power of sin, the flesh, and the world. But there's also a place for private prayer.

Daniel often retired to the little roof chamber above his home to have quiet time with God: "And he continued kneeling on his knees three times a day, praying and giving thanks before his God, as he had been doing previously" (Daniel 6:10).

Jesus said, "But you, when you pray, go into your inner room, and when you have shut your door, pray to your Father who is in secret, and your Father who sees in secret will repay you" (Matthew 6:6).

For confession. It's difficult to get personally right with God in the middle of a distracting crowd. Some things must be saved for God's ears, away from all disturbances. Some struggles are buried so deeply in our hearts that only the Holy Spirit Himself can properly express them before the Father. We may need quiet and solitude to get to that place of confession.

Peter stood around the edge of the courtyard fire, one eye on the upper room, trying to discern what was happening to Jesus. He kept another eye on the crew around him, trying not to be recognized. Three times he was accused of being a follower and friend of Jesus. Three times he denied it. The rooster's crows brought his failure to light, and immediately he wanted to be alone: "He went out and wept bitterly" (Matthew 26:75).

Our own failures will drive us to find our place to cry out to God.

For reflecting. Jonah had just completed a difficult ministry assign-ment. He had preached "repent or die" sermons to an ungodly city (Jonah 3). When he finished, he climbed up on a hill that over-looked the city. By himself, he waited for God to act and contem-plated the results of his ministry.

It seems to me that for many of us, keeping busy is a permanent pastime. We have a drive to insure that each moment is full of activ-ity. That's not difficult to accomplish. Busyness is easy. But busyness with a purpose is much more difficult.

We should yearn for time to contemplate the purpose, direction, success, and satisfaction of our bustling. Where are we heading? Is it all worthwhile?

For crying. One of the most moving scenes in the Bible comes after Joseph, sold into slavery as a boy by his brothers, has survived years of unjust imprisonment in Egypt. Finally, he manages to become prime minister. He hasn't heard a word from his family in more than twenty years. He doesn't know if his father's still alive. He doesn't know what's happened to his younger brother, Benjamin, the only other child of his deceased mother.

In God's providence, the brothers travel to Egypt and into his presence. They need to buy grain. While he recognizes them, they don't know who he is. So he tests their hearts to see if they've held onto their former attitudes.

All works well until Benjamin is brought to him. Then Joseph "hurried out for he was deeply stirred over his brother, and he sought a place to weep; and he entered his chamber and wept there" (Gene-sis 43:30).

There are times that warrant tears.

For dreaming. Direction in life can flow out of dreaming the "what ifs."

Circumstances crashed down on Saul of Tarsus. A great light struck him down while he was on his way to persecute some Chris-tians. He saw a vision of Jesus and received a commission to go and preach. For three days he was blind and neither ate nor drank. Then he was able to see again and was baptized into the faith.

Immediately he tried to enter the synagogues and preach that Jesus is the Messiah. Threats against his life ensued. He narrowly escaped town by being let down the side of a wall, hiding in a basket (Acts 9).

What did Saul do then? In Galatians 1:17 he reports, "I went away to Arabia."

He went out to the desert. He needed time to think about the events of the previous days. His life's goals were now completely reversed; he needed a chance to think and even dream through all the implications of the changes.

For receiving God's wisdom. To find God's opinion on a matter requires a season of seeking.

It wasn't in the middle of the Israeli camp that Moses received God's teaching but up on Mount Sinai, alone (Exodus 19:20). Just before that Moses was overwhelmed with his duties. It is Moses' father-in-law who spots the trouble in Exodus 18 and advises the solution. Moses needed to delegate the responsibility for handling the people's grievances. After doing that, he climbed the mountain to receive God's wisdom in the form of the Ten Commandments.

For making decisions. Why is it that time-share condo and vacuum cleaner salesmen force you to make an on-the-spot decision about buying their products? Because they know that if you think about it, they'll probably lose their sale. To wait and think about it improves almost every decision. The demand of prevailing voices can spell disaster.

Mark 15 tells the story of Pilate. He recognized the motive of envy in the chief priests' accusations against Jesus. And he knew Jesus was innocent of their charges. But, "wishing to satisfy the multitude, Pilate released Barabbas for them, and after having Jesus scourged, he delivered Him over to be crucified" (verse 15). Pilate's name is forever enshrined among the villains of history. How different things might have been if he'd had time alone, away from the crowd, to think through his crucial decision.

For getting lonely. Mom can be a real pain to a teenage daughter, until Mom isn't around for a day or two. Children can drive Mom up the wall, but by the second night away from them, she's ready to find out how they're doing.

Paul, the missionary apostle, sat in a cold Roman prison. Lonely, he wrote, "Only Luke is with me. Pick up Mark and bring him with you, for he is useful to me for service" (2 Timothy 4:11).

Mark? John Mark? Remember, Mark was the young relative of Paul's friend, Barnabas, who bombed out on the first missionary journey (Acts 13:13). In fact, he was such a disappointment that Paul refused to take him on the next trip, a decision that caused Barnabas to separate from Paul (Acts 15:36-40).

A Roman prison is a lonely place. So Paul called for Timothy and Mark. "Come before winter" was his final plea (2 Timothy 4:21).

Here are some suggestions for how to make privacy work for your family.

First, make sure every family member has space of his own. It's worth the time, effort, and money.

It's great if each child has a room of his own, but that's not always possible. Perhaps each could have a desk or desk drawer that's off-limits to all others. Maybe you can provide certain hours each week that are Missy's private time in the room—sister Trinka has to vacate the premises. Later, it's Trinka's turn.

Your wife needs space to herself too—a desk on one side of the bedroom or a special nook in the kitchen. With our older boys now out of the house, Janet gets an office room all to herself.

And don't forget yourself. Maybe it's a comfortable chair and a magazine rack or a shop in the garage. Or maybe the greens of a golf course.

Second, plan privacy for each family member. Don't expect privacy to just happen. Respect others' need for privacy by knocking before pushing open doors. Leave letters and diaries unopened. Don't listen in on phone calls.

Third, plan privacy for yourself. I have a built-in guarantee of private time each day—when I run. Once a month or so, I drive to the ocean or up to the mountains. I climb a hill, sit on a log, and relax. I've even been known to toss a sleeping bag in the truck and drive off into the wilderness.

My greatest thrill last spring was climbing a mountain in Nevada where I could stare in every direction and not see a speck of human life. That's being alone. I wouldn't want to live like that, but a brief break is exhilarating.

Fourth, make sure your family knows that private time is unaccountable time. They don't have to report to you everything they did. Encourage manners. Teach biblical principles. Instruct in common sense. Then throw out your cautions and trust them.

Fifth, learn how to make your time alone valuable. You can do this by shutting out the world. Close the door, turn off the TV, climb into a tree house.

Take an honest look at yourself. Most humans spend a good amount of time examining how they look physically. The rest of us needs scrutiny too. Look at your successes and failures. Review strengths, and admit weaknesses. Look at the future. Where will you be five years from now? Is that where you want to be?

Talk openly to God. Where is He in your life? Do you really seek His advice? Do you make Him part of all you do? Are you a thankful, grateful child of His?

Take time to appreciate the others in your sphere. Getting away from the family can help you think about them more. Think about how uniquely God has structured your family. Think about each one separately. You can do this by recording your thoughts, decisions, and ideas. Write them all down. Then share some with your family, if that seems like a good idea.

I once heard a lecturer say that in order to achieve our highest potential, we should spend at least 15 percent of our time just thinking. I don't know if he meant 15 percent of a twenty-four-hour day or a sixteen-hour day (since that's all the time we're awake). But even using the lower figure, that means a good two hours daily in thought. What a challenge for our action-oriented rather than thought-oriented society.

Our son Mike had a good summer job. And so, at age seventeen, he was left alone in our home while the rest of us took off on a month's vacation. Four weeks to himself. We left the freezer stuffed with frozen pizzas and the cupboards filled with soft drinks.

Weeks ahead we overheard him telling his friends about how he'd be on his own. One week after we left, I called him. I told him all about the Bear Tooth Mountains of southern Montana and the buffalo herd we'd driven through. Then I stopped long enough to ask him how things were at home.

"Actually, it's boring," he admitted. "Really boring."

That could be an important lesson for him to learn. He never would have learned it without being allowed some time to himself.

Privacy doesn't absolutely assure family harmony.

But it sure does help.

8

Caring Dads Are Zoo Keepers

To say Billy was a big kid was an understatement. He didn't play offensive lineman on the football team; he was the offensive line.

He stood in our kitchen next to a quickly-disappearing plate of chocolate chip cookies. His eating companion was the second largest kid on the team—my son Russell.

"Wow, Russ," Billy interjected between bites, "your family's really crazy! This place is like a zoo!"

Actually, I hadn't noticed anything unusual—except for the fact that the house was more crowded than usual. We had invited the entire high school senior class for lunch. And they came—all twenty-nine of them. They had piled into the first couple rows of our church that morning, and now they filled our home.

After Billy's comment, I surveyed the situation. A dozen or more kids played a video ski game in the basement family room. There, a chorus of shrieks and applause echoed at every well-executed turn.

Also in the basement, coming from Russell's room, a stereo blasted.

On the living room floor several girls lay on their backs engaged in an Indian leg-wrestling contest with fans cheering them on. The rest of the class played wilderness golf outside.

You've never heard of wilderness golf?

I had scraped out nine flat surfaces about two feet in diameter in the woods that surrounded our home, dug a hole in each, and stuck in short flags. Armed with golf clubs and plastic balls, players challenged the course by playing each shot where it lay.

Billy was right. It was a zoo.

I admit that I like it that way.

Billy's amazement grew out of the fact that his only previous contact with a Christian family had been through the media. TV, movies, and magazines didn't portray a very enticing picture of Christians. He assumed we'd be stiff, formal, puritanical holdovers from another century.

Jesus said He came to give us life—abundant life (John 10:10). We all know He came to call us to an eternity with Him, but the abundance He promised is for right now. That means an individual life and a family life that's full of purpose, meaning, and excitement. I think that means a family that's fun.

If we're going to build that kind of family, we not only need privacy, but we also need to nourish intimacy. Intimacy means time together. In Genesis 2:24 we're told, "A man shall leave his father and his mother, and shall cleave to his wife." That's what intimacy is all about: cleaving, holding on tight, not letting go.

But we're surrounded by enemies of intimacy. Here are some of the most common.

Missed meals. Eating is a personal experience. That's why when we invite guests for a meal, we tend to become much closer to them. Family life is the same. Every meal that has all family members present will act as a link to building bonds of intimacy.

The traditional picture of Mom, Dad, and kids sitting around a bountiful table is slipping away from many family units, and we're paying the price.

Uncomfortable living rooms. A strange idea? Not really. The simple fact is, if you don't have one room in the house with ample, cozy seating for every family member, you're not going to spend much time together.

Having each child in their rooms with doors closed is no more intimate than a college dorm or army barracks. One room's got to encourage fun or relaxation. And lack of money isn't the problem. Money can even enhance the problem. Expensive furnishings can hamper comfortable intimacy.

Uncontrolled schedules. A hard-working dad used to have the busiest schedule in the family. That description doesn't fit today. Missy has to go to the library, then to cheerleading practice, then to piano lessons. Meanwhile, Junior plays soccer, attends a Scout meeting, and takes judo lessons at the "Y."

Mom barely has time to get them there because she works at the gift store, does volunteer work at the hospital, and takes art classes.

Modern dads often come home to an empty house—it's hard to forge intimacy that way.

Skipped vacations. It's my personal conviction that a missed vacation drains part of a family's intimacy possibilities.

In our hectic roller-coaster life-styles, vacations aren't luxuries; they're necessities. They're one time in the year when a family disengages from the familiar ruts and launches out together on some great adventure.

A young couple cornered me after I'd spoken at a family conference. They had a dilemma. "How can we get our eight-year-old daughter and four-year-old son closer together? They barely know each other. They live in two separate worlds."

I know one thing that would assist. Plenty of family outings for just the four of them would provide fresh, new environments for relating.

Television. I don't have an anti-television crusade to promote. But let's be honest. When the TV's on, conversation's shushed, and the family's passive. It doesn't matter how good the programming. Whether it's news, sports, movies, cartoons, or Christian interviews, intimacy's inhibited.

The average home has the set turned on at least six hours per day. The average dad visits with his child less than fifteen minutes a day. It's not too difficult to figure out some of the consequences. In many homes the most common phrases between family members are

"What's on tonight?" and "Turn up the sound."

How does the Bible illustrate family intimacy? Let's look at some of the elements.

Long-term commitment. "But Ruth said, 'Do not urge me to leave you or turn back from following you; for where you go, I will go, and where you lodge, I will lodge. Your people shall be my people, and your God, my God. Where you die, I will die, and there will I be buried. Thus may the Lord do to me, and worse, if anything but death parts you and me' " (Ruth 1:16-17).

That's what you call long-term commitment. If that was the ideal for in-laws, such as Ruth and Naomi, how much more the standard for every Christian family.

Open-eyed forgiveness. Remember Jesus' parable about the prodigal? "And he got up and came to his father. But while he was still a long way off, his father saw him, and felt compassion for him, and ran and embraced him, and kissed him" (Luke 15:20).

That's not blind forgiveness that says, "My son can do no wrong."

True forgiveness grabs up a guilty, teary-eyed child who proclaims, "Daddy, I'll never ever do that again."

Mutual accountability. "Then the Lord said to Cain, 'Where is Abel your brother?' And he said, 'I do not know. Am I my brother's keeper?' " (Genesis 4:9). The obvious implication is, "Yes, you certainly are your brother's keeper!"

But, it's more than brother accountable to brother. It's kids accountable to parents and parents accountable to kids. Our demand for proper behavior from our children needs to follow our good role models.

Transmission of spiritual truth. The wise author of Proverbs 6:20 writes, "My son, observe the commandment of your father, and do not forsake the teaching of your mother."

Spiritual truth should emanate from the church, from the Sunday school teacher, from the preacher, and from independent studies. But parents should take the prime responsibility for instilling spiritual truth in their children. Children seldom forget the lessons they learn from the schooling at home.

Unwavering prayer. Job was a steadfast prayer. "And it came about, when the days of feasting had completed their cycle, that Job would send and consecrate them, rising up early in the morning and offering burnt offerings according to the number of them all; for Job said, 'Perhaps my sons have sinned and cursed God in their hearts.' Thus Job did continually" (Job 1:5).

Job was so concerned that each of his children had a right relationship with God that he constantly remembered them in his intercessions.

How can a caring dad encourage family intimacy? First, I've listed a sample set of rules that might act as your guide. Second, I'll share with you some fun things to try. These could be called the ten commandments of strong family life.

1. We will spend at least thirty minutes a day just talking. At mealtime, bedtime, anytime—everyone gets an opportunity to discuss what's on his mind, and we all learn how to listen to each other.

2. We will attempt to attend the activities of all other family members. Missy attends Junior's open house, and Junior sits through Missy's recital. Dad and the kids trail along when Mom collects her first-place ribbon at the Fine Arts Festival, and the whole family watches Dad compete in the racquetball finals.

3. We will refuse to put down another family member. It's an offense of the first level to make fun of a family member, in public or private.

4. We will plan a fun family activity once a month. Pencil in the dates at the first of the year and make these a top priority for everyone. Let all ages help in the planning. Set aside the necessary funds. Keep searching for activities that appeal to everyone.

5. We will establish a standard of ethics and behavior for the

whole family. For Christians, this standard comes from the Bible. But the specifics may need to be carefully explained at a family council meeting, as the need arises, according to the stages of each member.

6. We will establish our own family traditions. The uniqueness of your way of doing things gives your family a sense of identity. From huckleberry pies for Dad's birthday, to a family hike to the top of Mount Lassen each summer, to visiting the convalescent home each Mother's Day; from a special steak dinner to honor good grades, to picking out a yearly theme verse each January first, to spending Easter vacations doing missionary work, to decorating the Christmas tree on a given night—every family should create their own traditions.

7. We won't allow one family member to dominate every discussion. Each member needs to have his or her say. Even in areas where he has lesser knowledge, he should be made to feel important. Teach each one early that his opinions are valued.

8. We will watch for ways of letting another family member know we care. Quality families act as support personnel for one another. If Mom's the artist, she helps Missy with her student body campaign posters. Dad's on the lookout for a dress in Mom's "colors."

In our stressful world, we need all the help we can find. No matter how bad things get, it's cheering to know someone's rooting for you, wanting you to do the best you can.

9. We will try to make all major family decisions unanimous. Shall we move? Should we buy a car or a pickup? Do we want a dog or two cats? Should we go to Yellowstone or Malibu? Which church shall we attend?

Sometimes unanimity isn't possible. But it's surprising how often it can be achieved when it is sincerely sought.

10. We will work to build each member's expertise in at least one area. Mom's the music expert. Dad's the history buff. Missy's the

computer know-it-all. Junior knows more about reptiles than any-one. When birthdays and Christmas come around, we know the kinds of gifts they'll really enjoy. And nothing's more satisfying to a child than to know he has special skills or knowledge that he can add to the rest of the family.

Your family might have their own ideas to add or substitute to the previous list. An effective exercise would be to write your own set with some good discussion about what each means, then post them in a prominent place in the house.

All of this sounds like a lot of work. It is. But not all of these things have to be followed. Pick and choose according to your parti-cular family situation. And don't forget the fun. Here are some tested and proven ideas for promoting quality family fun.

Yearly family awards presentation. Ever watch the Oscar Awards on TV? Did you start to imagine what it would be like to hear your name called as a winner? What kind of acceptance speech would you give?

Why not try it at home? Set aside a formal affair night. Out come the linens, crystal, and china. Help Mom prepare a gourmet meal. Chip in for a good piece of meat. Buy some new candles or fresh flowers for the table.

Dad and boys wear their best Sunday outfits. Mom and the girls in dresses. Borrow a podium from the church, or dig out a music stand and set it up in your largest room. Have the chairs face the podium. Pull a floodlight from the patio. Put on some background music.

Then comes the good part. Assign each family member to present an award. They're to pick a category in which their assignee has ex-celled in the past year. Then they write a short speech to introduce them. One by one, you take the podium, introduce the category, de-scribe the nominee, and with appropriate fanfare ask for the envelope.

The winner proceeds to the podium with applause and gives an ac-ceptance speech. If you're creative enough, make a homemade trophy.

Imagine the excitement when Mom receives the The Best Cheerleading Outfit Seamstress with a Twenty-Four Hour Deadline award. Or Junior's pride as he accepts the Fastest Time in History Driving a Two-Wheeler Through the Sweet Peas award. He wants to thank his mother for planting the flowers, the Lord for helping the flowers grow, sister Missy for daring him to do it, and his dad for persuading him that it would not be in his best interest to ever do it again.

What does all this accomplish, besides a night of great fun and laughs? It builds intimacy. Shared experiences. Affirmation. Family unity. One of the world's best bargains.

Family Olympics. This works indoors or out. You might even want to do both. It can be done on vacation, as we've discovered while camping in the woods. Depending on the size and age of your family, have each member select several events. Include everything from pine cone toss, to wood chopping, to playing Monopoly, to running races, to picking up sticks, to cookie baking. Have at least ten different events. Then select a day for the competition, and make sure all the right gear is available.

Also, have each member make a small flag or banner as his personal symbol, to be solemnly raised at the gold medal presentations. In addition, each one could select a song to be sung as his personal anthem while receiving an award.

I'll never forget standing on a stump, waving my aspen bark flag with a crudely sketched buffalo, singing "Home, Home on the Range" after winning the boat races.

Blooper of the Year pantomime. This works great on New Year's Eve. Try to think of one event in which another family member made a blooper. Then pantomime it out for the other family members to guess.

Missy can act out Mom's reaction when the burnt toast set off the smoke alarm. Junior can portray Dad accidentally cutting through the outside Christmas lights while trimming the hedge. Dad can dance through the house in a starry-eyed gaze, as Missy after Randy asked to sit next to her at the school assembly. And Mom can imitate Junior hiding in the laundry hamper after Dad discovered his bent four wood.

My son Mike does a great pantomime of me. One time he demon-strated the way I responded when I realized I'd forgotten to close the back window of our Suburban and had lost Aaron's suitcase some-where in the middle of Oregon. This view of myself was actually humbling. My behavior was less than perfect, less than I expected of others. His act was humorous, but it also called me to account for my behavior. Accountability comes in many different forms.

Some activities don't need to be so elaborate. Next time you go to the airport or bus station to pick up a family member who's been gone awhile, gather up every friend of theirs with you. Pile them into the car, and make it a real welcome home party. Can you imagine what it does for one's ego to have a yelling, screaming gang surprise you at the terminal?

Buy or bum twenty feet of butcher paper and paint a gigantic greeting on it. Place it on the garage at home or spread it out as the traveler first appears. A fifteen-foot-long "Welcome Home! We Missed You!" is fun for everyone to see.

A simple thing we do around our house is give one another stand-ing ovations at special occasions. Janet's custard always receives such a response at the dinner table, as does anyone's memory verse. Thirty seconds of applause can make anyone's day.

It's possible to live in a family for twenty years and still grow up alone. It's more than sad; it's a tragedy. Caring dads won't let that happen. They'll turn their place into a zoo first, if that's what it takes.

9

Caring Dads Volunteer for the Christmas Play

"Now we need to have four angels," Karen Winston announced. She looked around at the entire Sunday School Department of Rock Creek Community Church. "All I need is four people who will wear white gowns and halos and recite in unison, 'Glory to God in the highest.' "

A hand shot up. "We'll take that one," Stan Richards called. "Marge, the girls, and I will be the angels."

Stan Richards, at 6 foot 4 inches tall, weighs a solid 250 pounds. His wife, Marge is a petite 5 foot 3 inches, and the two daughters are four and six years old. On Christmas eve they all dressed as angels. Stan's handlebar mustache added to the diversity.

Stan often volunteers his entire family for projects. When asked why, he replied, "As for me and my house, we will serve the Lord" (Joshua 24:15). "I figure that verse means that the father should lead his whole family in some type of service to the Lord," he further explained.

Stan has a point. Caring dads should look for ways to get family members involved in spiritual growth and service.

What are the marks of a spiritual home?

First, let's look at what a spiritual home is *not*. It is not a place

- where there's a pulpit in the living room, and all the chairs look like pews
- where the only time anyone raises their voice is to say "Praise the Lord!"
- where every family member is up, dressed, fed, and waiting anxiously in the living room a half-hour before Sunday school starts
- where the most often repeated phrase heard from the children is, "Yes, mother, I'd be happy to help out"
- where an exciting evening means sitting around the table playing "Name That Ancient Hymn"
- where every family member sits still during the prayer before meals, at times even begging Dad to pray longer
- where there are no unmade beds, dirty clothes tossed in closets, petrified spaghetti noodles in the pan in the sink, or half-eaten Christmas candy cane under the couch cushion
- where Missy spends every spare moment after junior high classes knitting socks for needy children overseas
- where Junior jumps up to turn off the TV when the cartoon show presents an unbiblical view of good and evil
- where the kids often invite their friends to come hear Dad's weekly morality lecture

A spiritual home? What is it really? The Bible gives us some guidelines.

First, a spiritual home encourages personal salvation.

"Behold, all souls are Mine; the soul of the father as well as the soul of the son is Mine. The soul who sins will die" (Ezekiel 18:4).

There is probably no greater assistance to a spiritual life than having Christian parents. Countless opportunities abound for hearing the truth of Jesus Christ. But each individual is responsible for his own spiritual commitment.

Christian parents can't force their children to believe. However, they can let them know how to become a Christian and help them understand they must make their own decision to accept Jesus Christ as Savior and Lord of their life. Our intense love for our children must never overshadow the fact they must take a stand for themselves. A caring, loving home can help nurture their desire to follow Christ.

Second, a spiritual home recognizes the Bible's authority.

"If anyone thinks he is a prophet or spiritual, let him recognize that the things which I write to you are the Lord's commandment" (1 Corinthians 14:37).

"All Scripture is inspired by God and profitable for teaching, for reproof, for correction, for training in righteousness" (2 Timothy 3:16).

Caring dads take the lead in establishing the Bible as the family's authority. Dad further demonstrates his belief by regular study and open obedience to its principles. Every family member is encouraged to read, study, memorize, and discuss Bible passages.

Third, a spiritual home develops a spiritual mind-set.

"For those who are according to the flesh set their minds on the things of the flesh, but those who are according to the Spirit, the things of the Spirit" (Romans 8:5).

That doesn't mean all your conversations must center on theological concerns. Nor does it mean that there is no laughter or humor. Spiritual homes can talk about world events, fall fashions, the latest toy fads, baseball games, and the cutest boy in the whole world that just moved in next door and asked Missy to go bike riding with him.

But whatever the main topic of discussion, talk about the Lord flows freely in and out, without awkwardness or embarrassment. Spiritual homes accept Jesus as Lord of every area of life, whether or not His Name is mentioned in a particular conversation.

Fourth, a spiritual home grows in spiritual understanding.

"And I, bretheren, could not speak to you as to spiritual men, but as to men of flesh, as to babes in Christ" (1 Corinthians 3:1).

We all start out as "babes in Christ." But He doesn't expect us to remain that way. We're supposed to grow and mature in spiritual knowledge and understanding. Dad should mature. Mom should mature. So should each child and the family as a whole.

Five years ago you might not have even considered asking the

Lord's wisdom to help you find a place for your vacation. This year you're praying together about it.

You might have lived next to the Montgomerys for three years, but just last week you got around to inviting them to church.

Two years ago you may have had no idea what the Bible said about issues like abortion or homosexuality. But now you know what you believe and why you believe it.

People in a spiritual home understand that they're not perfect. But the family desires to improve day by day, year by year. Problems stretch them. Mistakes keep them humble. Success gives them hope to keep going on.

Fifth, a spiritual home watches for spiritual implications.

"But he who is spiritual appraises all things" (1 Corinthians 2:15). Missy is pressured to attend a slumber party where a questionable movie will be shown, and the discussion goes deeper than Daddy's rules. It centers on how God's best can be produced in a young girl's life.

Two visitors at the door wearing dark suits and ties aren't just turned away because they belong to a cultic religious group. Dad can seize the opportunity to talk to the family about what their group's doctrine is based on and how that compares to the truth of Scripture.

Sixth, a spiritual home makes spiritual sacrifices.

"You also, as living stones, are being built up as a spiritual house for a holy priesthood, to offer up spiritual sacrifices acceptable to God through Jesus Christ" (1 Peter 2:5).

A few years ago a torrent of rain in the hills around our community poured water and mud down our canyon and busted through two hundred homes. Two and three feet of smelly debris stayed behind. It happened right before Easter vacation, and many church families—Dad, Mom, and kids—set aside their other plans to go down into the damaged housing development to shovel a week's worth of mud.

That's sacrifice.

Seventh, a spiritual home gently restores the fallen.

"Brethren, even if a man is caught in any trespass, you who are spiritual, restore such a one in a spirit of gentleness; each one looking to yourself, lest you too be tempted" (Galatians 6:1).

There are no perfect people, no perfect Christians, no perfect families on earth.

"We say that we have no sin, we are deceiving ourselves, and the truth is not in us" (1 John 1:8).

You can't expect your wife, daughter, son, or even yourself to exhibit flawless behavior, speech, motives, and actions every moment of the day. Some failures are certain. But, as the saying goes, they're never final.

"If we confess our sins, He is faithful and righteous to forgive us our sins and to cleanse us from all unrighteousness" (1 John 1:9).

You can be spiritual, striving for perfection. A family can be spiritual, struggling to reach perfection. Caring dads try to keep the environment loving and flexible enough to allow room for confession and restoration of each family member.

Eighth, a spiritual home cushions the needy.

"That is, that I may be encouraged together with you while among you, each of us by the other's faith, both yours and mine" (Romans 1:12).

The Christian is not free of trials, pain, suffering, grief, disappointments, doubts, struggles, and depressions.

Oh, we have our good times. We feel like we're walking hand in hand with our Lord. Our heart is content, our mind plots great things for God, our voices ring with His praises. At those times we think we can convert every heathen, raise every building fund, reverse every court decision, resolve every marriage conflict, and amaze every bored youth.

Then there are the other days. Sometimes we sob, "Why?" "Does God care?" "Where is He when I need Him?" "Does He really exist?" "I think I'll just give up. What's the use?" On these days, there's no substitute for a spiritual home.

I plopped down in my easy chair and let out a sigh. I was tired—tired of visiting, tired of planning, tired of trying to motivate others, tired of everything depending upon me for success at the church.

Most of all, I was tired with all the details of starting a new men's fellowship. After six years of trying to excite someone else to initiate it, I finally decided I'd have to do the work myself.

Now, just a few days before the first meeting, I wasn't sure it had all been worthwhile.

My son Mike walked into the room and flung himself down on the couch for a visit. I shared my problem with him.

"Well," he said, "I heard a preacher say once that you had to do the things in life you'd regret not doing. I suppose even if it fails you'd have regretted not trying. Right?"

I was the preacher he was quoting, and I desperately needed to hear my own message right then. Mike provided the words, and I gathered up strength and pushed on.

Even our kids have a way of refreshing us. Often, their timing is quite good.

Ninth, a spiritual home gives God recognition.

"Through Him then, let us continually offer up a sacrifice of praise to God, that is, the fruit of lips that give thanks to His name" (Hebrews 13:15).

A spiritual family thanks God for His provisions. Earlier I mentioned a time we lost Aaron's suitcase out of the back of our Suburban in the middle of Oregon. It was a bleak moment for me, feeling responsible for our three-year-old's losing all his clothes.

We prayed and prayed about finding the suitcase but had to give it up for vanished.

A week after we returned home from the vacation, I got a phone call from the local bus station. They had the suitcase there, sent by the Oregon police.

When I told Aaron the good news he ran out of the house to see his friends, yelling, "The Lord found my suitcase and sent it to me on a bus!"

His expression of joy revealed the right attitude. When tiny children are taught to give thanks to God for all He provides, such praise comes naturally.

Tenth, a spiritual home is never mediocre.

"Blessed be the God and Father of our Lord Jesus Christ, who has blessed us with every spiritual blessing in the heavenly places in Christ" (Ephesians 1:3).

There's nothing humdrum about receiving every spiritual blessing God has to offer. More families need to strive for excellence in their Christian commitment and service. Yes, we should enjoy life where we are. Yes, we each have unique families unlike any other. We don't want to copy someone else. But, at the same time, we should want to be the best we can be.

How can we be sure we're providing the atmosphere for quality family life?

First, accept the diversity of each family member as a strength. Make a list of each family member's strengths and acknowledge them as God's gifts to you through them. Commit each family member's weaknesses to God for His care and correction. Spend time thanking Him that it was His special design to bring all of you together.

Second, examine the basic spiritual environment from each family member's viewpoint. Does each family member feel relaxed at home? Are other members patient with him? Does he have fun times? Do you have any habits that prevent the spiritual growth of any member?

Pray for your family daily, that the power of this world's system, the power of their own fleshly desires, and the power of Satan be kept in check.

Third, be open with your own faith. Let your enjoyment of spiritual things spill over to your family. Don't just tell them to trust God in hard times. Let them see you doing it. Rejoice with them at the work God is doing in your life. Pull them into the secret dreams that you're depending on God to fulfill.

Building spirituality in a family can be fun.

One family I know likes to go to a costume shop during an off season and rent costumes for each family member. They suit up, and parade down to the pediatrics ward of the hospital or a nearby convalescent home. Imagine a hurting youngster's expression when in walks

Superman, Wonderwoman, a giant mouse, and a talking duck.

"Can you make me well, Superman?" a wide-eyed girl asked.

"No, but God can. Why don't we pray for His help?" came the reply.

The Majors have what they call their annual Thanksgiving Freeway Patrol. Since all their in-laws live out of state, they don't come to visit for the holidays. So Terry and Lisa Major cook a big dinner, turkey, pie, and all, put a table and patio chairs in the back of their pickup, and head out to the highway.

Terry's a mechanic with a full set of tools. They look for a family that's having car trouble and pull over to help. While Terry repairs the car, Lisa and their daughter set up the table and bring out the meal. They've even retained some lasting friendships through this ministry.

The Petersons live on Evergreen Drive. Most of the year it's a quiet, residential street. But for the three weeks before Christmas, it turns into the county show place for Christmas decorations. Every home for four blocks tries to outdo the neighbors with lights and scenes.

The Petersons join right in. They present a living manger scene, complete with borrowed sheep and donkey. The whole family takes turns playing Mary, Joseph, angels, wise men, and shepherds. One family member stands by the curb to distribute illustrated Scripture portions containing the Christmas narrative.

A spiritual home could be the most peaceful and comfortable and, at the same time, the craziest place on the block.

You never know what a spiritual dad will volunteer to do.

10

Caring Dads Make Them Pull Weeds

When we first moved to northern Idaho, our front yard consisted of nothing but weeds. They were nice weeds, since our house sat right in the middle of a forest. And at first, we didn't have a road or street leading up to the house, so our yard was full of natural vegetation.

Sooner or later, we had to tackle the yard. Mike, at fifteen, seemed a likely prospect to handle the job. But about five minutes after starting, he came back into the house. "I need some gloves," he reported.

That sounded reasonable to me. But he spent twenty minutes looking for gloves. After a brief time back in the yard, he returned again. "I've got to have some music," he informed me.

He spent fifteen minutes setting up his portable stereo on the front porch and trying to decide on the best tape for hoeing. Soon the pines swayed to the beat.

Ten minutes later I saw him again. "It's hot out there. I've got to have a drink."

A drink meant getting a large glass, plenty of ice, and mixing a pitcher of lemonade.

Finally, I thought I heard him chopping. But not for long. The front door opened, and he stood inside my study.

"Hey, Dad," he said, "you know what we need?"

"What's that?" I said, starting to get impatient.

"If we had one of those electric weed whips, I could buzz right over that whole yard in a matter of minutes. Otherwise, this'll take all day."

"Mike!" I began in my best drill sergeant's voice, "I don't care if it takes you all day, all week, or all month. You and that hoe are going to chop down every weed. Then you're going to rake them and carry them off. Now, stop stalling."

I'm sure I sounded insensitive to his struggles. But I did care. I cared enough to know that Mike, like all of us, needed to learn to put in a hard day's work.

I've never met anyone who knew how to work and wasn't taught that skill by some other person. Most humans begin life self-centered and leisure-centered. Caring dads teach good work habits.

It was taken for granted in biblical times that fathers took on this responsibility.

"A man had two sons, and he came to the first and said, 'Son, go work today in the vineyard.' And he answered and said, 'I will, sir;' and he did not go. And he came to the second and said the same thing. But he answered and said, 'I will not'; yet he afterward regretted it and went. Which of the two did the will of the father?" (Matthew 21:28-30). In this parable of Jesus, a father sent his sons to work—a very old precept.

How did you first learn to work? I had the privilege of growing up on a farm. I rode on Dad's lap on the tractor when I barely knew how to walk. I ran to keep up with him as he headed across an open field, shovel in hand. He'd cut down a worn out shovel and stick it in my hand so I could shovel too.

I learned how to prune plum trees, plant tomato seedlings, harvest walnuts, drive a cotton picker, repair packing house equipment, build spray rigs, plant orange trees, repair concrete pipe, pack bell peppers, dust vineyards, build greenhouses, and load produce trucks.

But not everyone has such an environment. Work on the family farm was a natural occurrence. You didn't stop to think about it, nor did you plan it out. It just happened.

Many careers today don't provide opportunities for teaching our children to work. In fact, we assume they ought to learn that kind of

thing at school. It should fit right in there with algebra, home eco-
nomics, and driver's education. But it doesn't.

Maybe we've forgotten some of the biblical principles behind the
"work ethic." God is not silent on such matters. Here's a quick review of what He has said.

First, God works.

"Thus the heavens and the earth were completed, and all their
hosts. And the seventh day God completed His work which He had
done; and He rested on the seventh day from all His work which He
had done" (Genesis 2:1-2).

The word *work* describes any physical or mental effort or activity
directed towards the production or accomplishment of something.
We don't want to anthropomorphize God (i.e., make Him like
man). Yet the Bible states that God worked and God rested. Not
only that, it says God is still working. "My Father is working until
now, and I Myself am working" (John 5:17).

Work is a divinely-instituted activity. The drudgery often con-
nected with it might be because of the sin of mankind. "Cursed is the
ground because of you; in toil you shall eat of it all the days of your
life" (Genesis 3:17).

Heaven is not going to provide absence from work but absence
from drudgery. In Luke 19:17 Jesus tells a parable of the heavenly reward of a faithful servant. "Well done, good slave, because you have
been faithful in a very little thing, be in authority over ten cities."

Authority over ten heavenly cities may not be the same as authority over ten earthly cities, but we get the idea we're not going to just
be lying around.

Work is a part of our creative nature. You and I would be miser-
able without it. The only difference I see between a present vocation
and retirement is that retirement allows more choices for the kind of
work you do.

Second, man is designed to work six days.

"You shall work six days, but on the seventh day you shall rest;
even during plowing time and harvest you shall rest" (Exodus 34:21).

The seven-day week is still one of the puzzles of the modern athe-

istic mind. Historians, socialists, and psychologists try to provide ex-
planations for the adoption of the seven-day week. You can chart
days by the earth's rotation, months by the moon, and years by the
earth's journey around the sun. But a seven-day week remains a
mystery.

It's no mystery to people of faith. God established the pattern. He
kept to that schedule Himself, as an example to us. On the seventh
day He rested (Genesis 2:2).

We're to work, and we're to rest. Many people don't know how to
put in six hard working days. In fact, many feel unfairly treated and
work only a five-day week. Others don't know how to have a day of
rest. The biblical view requires us to learn how to do both.

Caring dads teach by example and training what it's like to stick to
a work project from morning to night, day after day. But they also
teach, by example, how to get the most out of a day of rest and
worship.

Third, God appoints specialized work skills.

"Now Bezalel and Oholiab, and every skillful person in whom the
Lord has put skill and understanding to know how to perform all the
work in the construction of the sanctuary, shall perform in accor-
dance with all that the Lord has commanded" (Exodus 36:1).

We can learn all about a subject, take all the training courses,
even survive the apprenticeship, but still fail to be successful with a
particular job or occupation. Not everyone can do everything. Our
education and training is meant to pull together those natural talents
we were given, to coordinate them in a work that satisfies our full
potential.

This verse in Exodus tells about the special skills given to two
craftsmen. Our children, too, have specialized gifts and talents. You
may already recognize some of them. Caring dads encourage the education and training that nourishes those talents to the satisfaction of
the child. Junior may not have the same talents you do and may not
want to take over the family business. While we don't select our
child's profession, we want to give them opportunities to find out
who they are.

Fourth, work has rewards.

"But you, be strong and do not lose courage, for there is reward for your work" (2 Chronicles 15:7).

King Asa needed this encouraging word from the prophet Azariah. The people of Judah were surrounded by many powerful and fierce enemies. By casting all his trust in the Lord, Asa had just completed a successful battle against the Ethiopians (2 Chronicles 14:12). But more battles would come.

Questions must have remained in his mind, such as, "Is all of this continual struggle worthwhile?" "Where's it leading us?" Even, perhaps, "I'm too tired, too tense to go through this again."

The reply comes clear and direct: "Hang in there; it's all worth it."

This principle applies to our present workdays. While few of us are given a position of leading an entire family of faith, we're busy doing the individual work task assigned to us. We, too, feel crunched at times. We need to remember that work has its rewards.

Children should learn at an early age that work pays the bills. The heat from the furnace, the pie on the stove, and the new birthday shoes are due to someone's work.

There's also the reward in achievement. A field plowed, a report finished, a sale made, a fire extinguished, a student taught—all bring enjoyment to the worker.

In addition, there's the positive effect on the personal needs of the worker. You perfect a skill. You learn something new. You accomplish something you didn't know you could do. You strengthen a relationship. All these help you appreciate God's gifts to you.

Fifth, work needs follow through.

"And the men did the work faithfully" (2 Chronicles 34:12).

What kind of men are being described in this passage? Carpenters, stone masons, lumberjacks, and "burden bearers" (i.e., common manual laborers). Honest work means doing exactly what we said we would do.

If Junior says he's going to mow the lawn by noon, you help teach him to keep that commitment. If Missy promises to wash dishes for a week, you don't let her stop after three days. If Joey wants to take on a paper route, he goes out even in the rain.

A few months before my oldest son, Russ, got married, he secured a good job as an equipment operator in the construction business. That kind of position allowed him to support a wife, and it also meant rising early and trudging off to work day after day.

After a few weeks on the job, someone offered him baseball playoff tickets. Being a fanatic sports fan, he was tempted to take off work to see the game. A few buddies told him to just call in sick. But he amazed us all by giving up the tickets and plugging away on the job. It was one of the signs that began to convince me that, indeed, this twenty-year-old son was mature enough to get married.

Sixth, a good day's work begins in the mind.

"So we built the wall and the whole wall was joined together to half its height, for the people had a mind to work" (Nehemiah 4:6).

Let's face it, on some days you get a lot more accomplished than on others. Of course, we have many unforeseen problems to overcome. There are times when it seems our whole things-to-do list has been undermined by circumstances. But I've found I'll get done what I set my mind to, and rarely more.

For a pastor, interruptions are a way of life. It's unrealistic to plan to have a whole day to myself, exactly as scheduled. It's never happened. But my productivity depends upon how I choose to handle those intrusions.

Yesterday I determined to complete one chapter of this book. As I typed at my desk, I had a dozen phone calls, seven unexpected visits, and one real crisis. Yet I completed the chapter.

I handled the ordinary matters quickly, postponed whatever I could, and made a quick trip to the hospital for a visit. At 8:30 that evening I typed the last sentence.

Some days the claims on my time would have so disoriented me that I would have given up quickly, putting the whole project off to another day. The difference was my mind-set. I decided that nothing would keep me from it.

Seventh, work should equal pay.

"The worker is worthy of his support" (Matthew 10:10).

There are two ways of looking at this verse. First, we need to live up to our wages. We should view our work as a contract (usually verbal) by which we promise to deliver a certain amount of effort in return for a certain amount of goods, services, or provisions.

But, further, this verse reminds us that we deserve to get paid for the work that we do. That's the difference between work and a free gift. Children should, and do, receive many free gifts. That's part of the love relationship between parent and child. But they should also learn that certain work done earns a material reward. Then allow them to use their pay the way they choose.

Last spring our son Mike wanted to buy a car. He called me one day to tell me he'd found a great deal on a four-wheel-drive Jeep. But he had to decide right away. That evening, I took a look at the Jeep. Together, we went over how many things would have to be repaired. I showed him the total cost, the obvious faults, and cautioned him about unknowns. Then I allowed him to make the final decision. He needed to learn—the hard way.

Eighth, work is the Christian norm.

"And to make it your ambition to lead a quiet life and attend to your own business and work with your hands, just as we commanded you" (1 Thessalonians 4:11).

The early church was plagued with two kinds of loafers. They were sincere in their commitment to Christ, but in their daily living they misapplied Christ's teaching.

One group was so convinced that the Lord would be returning anytime that they quit their jobs, moved up to a hillside, and waited. Naturally, they got hungry. Soon they had to sponge off their families. A second group noticed the generosity of those first-century believers and decided to take in a free meal or two, which led to a type of Christian welfare life-style.

Christians should not be this way, Paul insists. Just do your work, don't complain, and earn your own way.

What a refreshing viewpoint. Imagine a worker that bothers no other workers, always puts in a steady day's work, doesn't complain, and can be counted on to fulfill everything assigned to him. He would definitely be an employee a boss would remember.

It's important that workers, whatever the age, remember that their ultimate purpose is not to extract more and more money for less and less work, but rather to expand the kingdom of God by being a witness of His love and saving power.

Ninth, the able must work.

"For even when we were with you, we used to give you this order: if anyone will not work, neither let him eat" (2 Thessalonians 3:10).

Christian generosity is world reknown. James equates lack of charity with lack of saving faith. "If a brother or sister is without clothing and in need of daily food, and one of you says to them, 'Go in peace, be warmed and be filled,' and yet you do not give them what is necessary for their body, what use is that?" (2:15-16).

While the widows, orphans, and helpless must be provided for, the able-bodied are required to work.

A few years ago I happened to wander to the back of the house right before supper. My oldest boys, then sixteen and nineteen, had evidently not learned the complicated skills required for making their beds, putting away their clothes, and straightening their rooms. I decided it was time to apply 2 Thessalonians 3:10. I told them there was no supper until the rooms were cleaned up. No work, no food.

How do we instill these vital habits in our children as they grow up? Perhaps you could develop one of the following ideas to fit your own situation.

- Make a list of those once- or twice-a-year jobs that need to be done around the house and yard and decide on the amount you'd be willing to pay for them. Let the kids choose which they want to do. Make sure each job is adequately described and a time limit is given for completion.

- Sign up the whole gang for a church or community work day. Offer your kids a certain wage (or this may be the time for them to learn about volunteer work), and then complete the project while you work alongside them. If your church has no such work day, then call the church office and volunteer anyway.

- Go camping or to a backwoods cabin. Divide up the chores of splitting wood, carrying water, and cleaning up. Assign the work details, then rotate the jobs.

- Check your area for a food-share program. Some farmers, packers, and shippers are stuck with extra produce and food items. The food-share group is given permission to pick, unpack, or sort through the items. They can keep half for themselves and give half to an organization that feeds the poor and needy. It can provide a hard but rewarding day's work for the whole family.
- Grow a garden. It's worth it if for no other reason than it teaches kids responsibility and work. Take out some of the ivy, lawn, or decorative rocks and plant tomatoes, beans, and squash instead. If you don't have the space, check around town for community garden sites where you can do your amateur farming.

Caring dads look for ways to put their children to work. Not out of perverse delight in seeing them struggle and sweat, but because they know some lessons can't be learned any other way.

11

Caring Dads Marry Them Off

Jan and I had just spent a week hopping around the Midwest. We'd done some speaking and radio interviews, and we were ready to get back home. Being a country boy, there are two things I miss when away from home: one is the wide, open spaces, and the other is my family. I openly confess to being a familiholic.

We were anxious to greet our sons, who had to drive two hours from our Idaho home to pick us up at the Spokane airport. As we came down from the ramp, I scanned the crowded terminal for a glimpse of Russ and Mike. Since they're both over six feet tall, I figured they'd be easy to spot. Right away I saw Russ. We headed his way. But I couldn't see Mike anywhere.

Then, all of a sudden, someone else came into view. A girl next to Russ? We'd only been gone six days. There had been no girl friend when we left. My mind flashed back as we walked up to them.

Long brown hair, nice smile—oh, yes, she's from the youth group at the church. But when did they get serious? Or are they serious? Of course they're serious. It takes two hours to get here in the car—

She's a nice girl and a Christian, but I don't know her parents. They do make a cute couple, though. I wonder what she sees in Russ? No, I mean, I wonder how compatible they are? They look happy, but I know how it is—day in and day out, married life can be tough.

I wonder if she'd be content with such a laid-back husband. He does like children—probably be a good father. That's important. I hope she'll be a good mother. Hey, I wonder what my grandkids will look like?

My thought process lasted less than fifty seconds and fifty feet of terminal space. Russ interrupted with, "Hi, Dad, this is Suzanne."

I just have this habit of marrying my sons off in my mind. But Suzanne wasn't the one for Russ. After Suzanne came others.

Caring dads are actively concerned about their child's future mate. That's the way Bible dads were.

Abraham demonstrated the attitude of a caring dad. Of course, he may have had more at stake. He's the one the Lord called to leave his homeland and search for the Promised Land, where a whole nation of chosen people would settle. When he arrived there, the land was filled with a godless and immoral people. According to God's plan it would be a future generation, not Abraham's, that would finally conquer this people and possess the land. In the meantime, Abraham and his family faithfully served God and enjoyed His goodness to them.

Abraham's promise from God was to be kept alive through his family, which consisted of one son, Isaac. Isaac's wife would be very important to the history of this people of faith. And Abraham had some specific ideas.

Following the custom of the day, he described to his chief servant the kind of woman Isaac should marry. "I will make you swear by the Lord, the God of heaven and the God of earth, that you shall not take a wife for my son from the daughters of the Canaanites, among whom I live, but you shall go to my country and to my relatives, and take a wife for my son Isaac" (Genesis 24:3-4).

Rebekah and Isaac were part of the crucial genealogy of Jesus (Matthew 1:1-17). While my own daughters-in-law will not fit that same category, they certainly will be influential people in the redemptive plan of my grandchildren and their children. Therefore, it's with as much concern as Abraham that I consider my sons' future wives. I have my own set of guidelines. It's never too early to show your interest.

Age 0: Pray for your child's salvation, vocation, and future spouse. I remember the day I began to pray for Aaron, our five-year-old.

Janet returned home, sick, from a writer's conference. She moped around for several weeks, then announced she was going to purchase one of those home pregnancy tests. I assured her that her suspicion was ridiculous. After all, our sons were sixteen and thirteen. We were pushing forty—

But there it was—a telltale ring in a test tube, later confirmed by the doctor. On December 30 of that year, Aaron joined the Bly family. By then, I had prayed for him for months. I prayed for his sensitivity to the knowledge of God. I prayed that he would find a vocation that would use his God-given talents for the expansion of Christ's kingdom. I prayed that his future spouse would love the Lord God, complement my child's ministry and personality, and possess the necessary graces to raise my grandchildren. I still pray for all those things.

Age 2: Guard against outside influences. During the early years, we have tremendous control over most of our child's environment, including the people they come in contact with. We can choose their friends, the parties they attend, the neighbors who share their sandbox.

Billy Joe was the same age as our son Russell. But their backgrounds were worlds apart. The most violent scene Russ had encountered was a stray cat scratching his cheek. Billy Joe had spent those first few years of his life watching his drunken father slug his mother. For him, every disagreement ended with ear-splitting curses or eye-splitting punches.

One day we caught Billy Joe in Russell's bedroom, raging over the loss of a game. He had tried to bash Russ over the head with a baseball bat.

Billy Joe needed help. But our son wasn't a professional counselor. From then on, we severely curtailed their play times and then allowed them only under close supervision.

Age 4: Present a positive model. You're the only husband your child knows very well. Your little one knows you even better than you'd prefer. He hears everything you say, all the things you imply, and how you react in various daily interactions. For him, a husband is just like Dad; a wife is just like Mom.

Bryce was incensed when his teenage daughter's boyfriend pulled into the driveway and honked his horn rather than coming to the door. "Cindy, why do you go out with someone so rude?" he questioned.

"It's no big thing," she huffed. "You get impatient when Mom takes a long time, then go out and sit in the car to wait for her—what's the difference?"

Age 6: Teach biblical truth. They're not too young to grasp principles about love, marriage, and mates. We only put off such instructions because we're embarrassed or lazy.

Kelly's eight and playing the part of the princess in the school play. When Derrick was selected as the prince, she asked him if he was a Christian. "What difference does that make?" he asked.

"Oh, I don't want to marry anyone who doesn't know Jesus," she answered. Kelly had already been taught.

Age 12: Insist on boundaries. Establish the rules before they're even needed. If we wait until there's a problem situation, it will seem like we're picking on a particular friend.

Amy is just eleven, but she can hardly wait until she's sixteen. That's when her parents agreed she could date. She knows now that she can't leave the house without telling them where she's going, who she's going with, and when she'll be home. Mom or Dad have to meet her friends, too. Amy realizes these rules will continue through high school. She's establishing the habit early.

Age 16: Affirm correct choices and give loving warnings. By this time, our power to choose our children's friends fades. But we can encourage them when they make good choices. And we don't need to hesitate, when we sense danger signals, to speak up.

Be honest. Give a reasonable account of your misgivings. Kids see right through trumped up accusations to cover our prejudices. The quality of their friends' car, the location of their houses, and their parents' social standings may not be of prime importance.

It was tough, but I knew I had to talk to one of my sons about his girl friend. "You're too young for such a possessive relationship," I pointed out. "You're both still trying to discover who you are, how you relate, and what you want in life. You're not giving each other a chance to develop in other areas."

He didn't say a word. But three weeks later he marched into the living room and said, "Well, we broke up today—you know, I just need a little more freedom."

Age 18: Allow God to lead. Our direct involvement in their decisions should be limited. It's time to sit back, pray, and give them the reins.

For two summers Russell, our oldest, served on the staff of a large Christian campground, hundreds of miles from home. His mother and I prayed a lot. Midway through the second summer we got "the call."

"I've met this perfect girl, Dad. We get along great. Say, what do you think if I get married and not go to college after all?"

We traveled 350 miles to meet the object of his affections, all the while wondering what kind of situation we'd encounter. We loved her from first sight. We still do. Lois has made a delightful daughter-in-law.

Adult: Support their decisions. From the point of conception, we as parents can't help dream about our children's future. We plot their occupations. We save for their college education. We visualize their weddings and their spouses.

However, God has His own game plan. It doesn't always agree with ours. When we see our personal plans crumble, but His ultimately carried out, let's rejoice and cooperate with Him the best we can.

I figured Russell would go to the university, major in computer science, and work in the Silicon Valley. At twenty, he married and became a heavy equipment operator. Dear old Dad couldn't be happier—or prouder.

The seasons come and go. Our roles change. I no longer tell my oldest to clean his room, keep his elbows off the table, or stand to seat the ladies. But I'll crawl under his house to help him fix the plumbing. Or I'll listen to his struggles to get along with a difficult foreman. Or offer my opinion on where to invest bonus money.

Meanwhile he has the freedom to make some mistakes, and he knows I'll be there. He knows I feel that way about his wife, too.

My attention to them hasn't diminished, even though the intensity of my concern is now directed toward my middle son, Mike.

"I hear Patty is sorry that we broke up." Mike, as a high school senior, reported on his latest romance. "I guess they're all sort of sorry."

"Oh?" I said as I gave him an interested, fatherly glance, then continued fixing the garage door.

"I mean, Megan's still upset over our breakup last January. And I know Karla wishes we hadn't stopped dating last July. And now, Patty—"

I tried not to let my grin seem too obvious. "Sounds like you're doing some reconsidering," I offered. "Well, which one interests you the most?"

"Crystal Flannery," he said, without hesitation.

"Crystal Flannery!" I echoed. I hadn't heard that name since sixth grade. She used to be the skinny little girl with barrettes. Now she was head cheerleader and homecoming queen.

It's tough being the father of a high schooler and even tougher when they go off to college. I'd like to personally inspect and consider each steady date in light of their candidacy as my future daughter-in-law. But Mike moves so fast I hardly learn their names. That's all right, because I'm in no hurry. But I'm constantly reminded of the importance of choosing lifelong mates. I want the best situation for each child at each stage of the relationship.

Caring dads walk a tenuous balance beam. We must instruct, guide, lead, suggest, and nudge. Yet we can't force, insist, or dictate.

12

Caring Dads Cry
When They Leave Home

Grown men don't cry.

Ever.

That was part of the unwritten and unspoken code when I grew up. It doesn't matter whether your dog gets killed, someone steals your baseball mitt, or your sister eats the last piece of pecan pie—big boys don't cry.

There are advantages to that philosophy. For instance, it's tough to get things done when you're busy getting teary and grabbing for handkerchiefs. So even if you drop a bushel of tomatoes on your foot, have to listen to a coach's tirade, or get knocked flat during a basketball game, you just keep right on going.

Ten years ago my dad died. He was only sixty-one. I'm his only son, the one who used to be a farmer—now the minister. So I remained strong and unemotional during all the arrangements. After all, I had to comfort the women. I needed to show strength for my mother, my sister, my wife.

I had officiated dozens of funerals. I knew what to expect, what to do, how to respond. "He took it so well" was the standard I strived for.

Months later I loosened up. Not that I let anybody know, of

course, but there was a day or two of closing the bedroom door to shed some heart-relieving sobs of loneliness and grief. Some things in life are worth a cry. My dad's death was one of them.

What a phony delusion we have of real humanity. To show your emotions—your tears—to those you love is not a sign of weakness, but a sign of strong love.

I got a phone call from Terry's aunt. I barely knew her, and I hadn't seen Terry in years. She informed me that Terry had died suddenly, and the family wanted me to do the funeral service. I agreed.

When I was a teenager, busy with sports, girls, and cars, Terry had lived across the street. He was not more than three or four at the time, but he had insisted on joining the bigger kids' games. He was a lovable but tough little nuisance. Most days he'd get shoved aside and be told to go home. But he hung in there and eventually developed into an excellent athlete.

He played quarterback for the high school and college teams, a popular man around campus. After college, he continued to draw many around him and was engaged to be married. Just three weeks before the wedding his parents returned home to find him dead on the living room floor. An autopsy revealed a brain tumor no one knew existed. Terry was gone.

I knew it would be a difficult service. His age and popularity meant a big crowd. The rows were jammed, the aisles were filled, the entryway overflowed, and a number stood outside the front door.

I had to speak loudly to be heard. Not just because of the crowd but because of the sobs of the father. It was understandable for a man to feel such grief. A number of times I had to wait for his wails to quiet down before I resumed.

What a sad day. But the saddest part looms in my memory when Terry's father admitted later that he'd never once shown Terry such emotion. They hadn't hugged since Terry was a baby, because men didn't hug each other. He'd never cried in Terry's presence, never looked him in the eye and said, "I love you." It had always been a nice, unemotional relationship.

The biblical view of a man's relationship with his family is quite different. Most experts agree that the Old Testament records the history of a patriarchal society. It was a man's world, one where husbands and fathers had the ultimate say and the final responsibility. Yet there were times when only tears could express the feeling of the heart.

After years of heart-breaking separation from his family, Joseph was reunited not only with his brothers but with his father as well. What happened then? "And Joseph prepared his chariot and went up to Goshen to meet his father Israel [Jacob]; as soon as he appeared before him, he fell on his neck and wept on his neck for a long time" (Genesis 46:29).

Jesus was not a wimp. Any picture that depicts him as such is wrong and boarders on idolatry (that is, offers a false image of the Divine.) He was the kind of man who needed only to speak, "Follow Me," and men left everything to be by His side.

He looked at a hostile crowd, and they backed away. He walked up to a demon-possessed man who had overcome dozens of strong men, and everyone recognized that He was in charge. Kings, governors, centurions, and supreme court officials could not impress or control Him. When He grabbed up the whip to chase off the money changers, everyone knew that this was one man you didn't tangle with.

Yet twice Scripture records that Jesus wept.

In John 11:33 and following, we find the account of the death of His good friend Lazarus. When He sees Lazarus's sisters' tears, He empathizes so deeply that tears come to His eyes as well. Even though He knows that in a few minutes He'll raise Lazarus from the dead, at that moment He hurts.

In Luke 19:41, Jesus approaches Jerusalem for the last time. The crowds shout, "Hosanna," but Jesus cries, "If you had known in this day, even you, the things which make for peace!" (verse 42).

There's no question that out of all the cities of the earth, Jerusalem was closest to Jesus' heart. There, where they should have received Him as Messiah, they would soon reject and crucify Him. That action would generate long-range effects, which included His accurate prediction of the city's destruction (Luke 21:6). Jerusalem's rebellion drove Him to tears.

The point is, for Jesus or Joseph, for you or me, there are some things in life worth crying about. It's not manly to hold in all emotions. It's not human, and it's even harmful. Our children deserve to know how much they mean to us.

Here are some of the things that make caring Dads weep.

First, at the reunions of separated family members.

"Then Esau ran to meet him and embraced him, and fell on his neck and kissed him, and they wept" (Genesis 33:4).

The twin brothers, Jacob and Esau, had been estranged for years. The point of contention had been Jacob's deception at Esau's expense. Jacob had won the birthright in a spur-of-the-moment barter, then stolen Esau's blessing. He fled the land because of Esau's threat to kill him—not what you'd call a strong brotherly bond.

But many years later, Jacob wanted to come home. He approached Esau with fear and trembling. He tried to soften the meeting with presents, then introduced his family and wealth. Finally, there was nothing left to do but meet Esau alone, face-to-face. We know little about Esau during the time of separation, except that he obviously had done some mellowing. We see two brothers, together again, weeping and embracing.

Families were meant to be united. It's not natural or helpful to have barriers between brothers and sisters, parents and children, husband and wife.

Sherry's voice broke with emotion. She couldn't finish making her prayer request to the Sunday night fellowship. Finally the words spilled out.

For six years her parents had refused to speak to her. They wouldn't write or open her letters. She was heartsick. She wanted reconciliation, but they wouldn't even consider it. Caring dads not only work for the reuniting of family members; they even shed a tear or two when unity is restored.

Second, at the deaths of family members. There's no debate that Jacob loved his son Joseph. And there's no mistaking that Joseph felt the same way.

In his younger days, Joseph's special place was in his father's heart, and his own arrogance alienated his brothers. They retaliated by selling Joseph to traveling merchants and telling Jacob that Joseph was dead.

Jacob, stricken with grief, could not be comforted. "Surely I will go down to Sheol in mourning for my son" (Genesis 37:35).

Joseph wasn't really dead, and many years later there was a tearful reunion. Later, Jacob's time came to die. This time Joseph wept. "Then Joseph fell on his father's face, and wept over him and kissed him" (Genesis 50:1).

Many men believe such a thing shouldn't be done, especially in public. But that's unreal. If you hurt, why pretend that you don't? If you're overcome with sorrow at a loss, why not share that with someone? Crying is the outward sign that you love, you care. To admit that is the best part of being human.

Sometimes Christians have a hard time with grief at the death of a loved one. We say, "Well, I know they're better off," or, "I'm sure they're happy now." But such sentiments don't deal with our hearts. If we hurt, we hurt. We're going to miss that person, and no one else can take their place. There are times to let the tears flow.

Third, when sinners repent. Joseph wasn't a crybaby. He was prime minister of Egypt. He had to earn his position the hard way, by serving as a common slave and filling out a prison term. He did this in a foreign country, far from family.

When he saw his brothers again after all those years, he needed to know if they'd changed. Would they still stab him in the back? When he discovered their new attitudes, he wept (Genesis 50:17).

Too often our goal for those who wrong us is revenge or punishment. We may even oppose their repentance because we don't want to see them get away with something. Caring dads concern themselves with people rather than retribution.

Fourth, at the final parting of good friends. David and Jonathan provide a classic example of good friendship. But they had to separate because of Jonathan's father's unceasing campaign against David. They knew they could no longer see each other, except from opposite sides of the battlefield. First Samuel 19:41 records the scene:

"When the lad was gone, David rose from the south side and fell on his face to the ground, and bowed three times. And they kissed each other and wept together, but David more."

Unmanly? How could it be? They were two of the mightiest fighting men the Hebrew people produced.

When you help the next-door neighbors load their moving van and wave to them as they make their final exit down the street, it's all right for Junior—or even you—to let the tears roll.

When you have a going-away reception at the church for a missionary couple, it's natural to feel the tug at your heart. Caring dads are deeply touched at the parting of good friends.

Fifth, at the loss of valued possessions. Our happiness isn't solely tied to what we own. Our trust and joy should be based on our relationship with the Lord God. But we do enjoy God's good gifts to us, and we want to be good caretakers of them. It's not spiritual to disregard all our belongings.

When David and his men returned to their home town and found the city a burning pile of rubble and their families carried off by raiders from the desert, they reacted in a perfectly acceptable manner. They "lifted their voices and wept until there was no strength in them to weep" (1 Samuel 30:4).

I sloshed through three feet of water to reach the McIntosh's front door. Nick sat up on the hood of his less-than-two-week-old car, now completely ruined. Three feet of mud filled their home. Everything from appliances to piano, from clothes to antiques, even family photo albums were lost forever.

I was overwhelmed with the devastation. "What can I do, Nick?" I struggled to say.

He shook his head. "There's nothing left but to cry."

Sixth, at the serious illness of a child.

"While the child was still alive, I fasted and wept" (2 Samuel 12:22).

There was trouble at the birth of the little one, the firstborn of David and Bathsheba. David prayed for him for seven days and nights.

Take a walk through the pediatrics ward of the hospital. Ask to visit the terminally ill. Then tell me how stoic you are, how much in control of your emotions, how brave and manly not to weep.

When David's baby died, David stopped weeping. "I shall go to him, but he will not return to me" (2 Samuel 12:23). There's a time to weep and a time to stop weeping. Caring dads know when and how to do both.

Seventh, over rebellious children. King David had a large family. With several wives and many children, it's hard for us to sort out the whole gang. But David knew them all.

One son especially captured his father's heart: Absalom. He seemed to have the leadership style and charisma of the young David. But he's best known to us for his rebellion against his father in trying to take over the kingdom for himself. He almost succeeded.

David chose to leave Jerusalem rather than spill family blood. "And David went up the ascent of the Mount of Olives, and wept as he went, and his head was covered and he walked barefoot" (2 Samuel 15:30).

Did he cry about losing his kingship? Perhaps. But it's more likely that he mourned the lost relationship with his son.

David never disowned Absalom. When his own army closed in, he pleaded with his generals, "Deal gently for my sake with the young man Absalom" (2 Samuel 18:5).

When he heard of his death, he cried out, "O my son Absalom, my son, my son Absalom! Would I had died instead of you, O Absalom, my son, my son!" (2 Samuel 18:33).

Eighth, when he fails God. You and I know lots of guys like Peter. We vote them captain of the football team, jury foreman, and head of the building committee. They're the guys that get the job done. They're strong, impetuous, full of pride, and self-assured.

When Jesus warned of the upcoming harsh times, he prophecied that all the disciples would flee and hide. Peter insisted that he'd stick with Jesus no matter what. "Even though all may fall away because of You, I will never fall away," he boasts in Matthew 26:33.

But Peter denied Christ—which caused him to weep bitterly.

Our sins should drive us to our knees in tears. If they don't, we must not understand the seriousness of our offense, nor the depth of the price Christ paid to allow us such a treasure as forgiveness. Caring dads weep over their failures.

Ninth, for the poor, oppressed, and needy. Job spent a lot of time examining his life, trying to figure out what went wrong. He inspected his past actions. "Have I not wept for the one whose life is hard? Was not my soul grieved for the needy?" (Job 30:25).

That's the proper attitude: true grief—real tears—shed because of life's tragedies.

Tenth, for those who've turned away from the faith. Refusing to follow Christ is a greater disaster than losing a life. When that dawns on us, then sorrow and tears should flow for those who disregard God's appeals.

Paul wrote, "For many walk, of whom I often told you, and now tell you even weeping, that they are enemies of the cross of Christ" (Philippians 3:18).

But there are other ways of expressing our emotions—tears aren't the only means of communication. Here are some other ways you show your love for your family.

You can tell them. Simple enough. Just look them in the eye, smile, and say, "I love you." It doesn't matter whether your children are boys or girls, five or fifteen, whether you just saw them this morning or haven't seen them in years. Tell them you love them.

A man grabbed my arm after a conference and wanted to talk. He had a difficult time showing affection to his twelve-year-old son. "I've always been taught that men only said those things to a woman. You know what I mean? He'd just get embarrassed and leave the room if I said anything like that."

For some, it is awkward. I've been saying that to our sons for a lot of years, so it comes naturally. We call Mike every Sunday night while he's away at college. I always end the conversation with, "We love you." Corny? Not if I mean it and not if a son far away from home needs reminding.

You can hug them. In some families and cultures, it's a standard custom to hug family members when you greet them or leave them. I
envy such folks. Hugging isn't easy for me. It's taken a lot of practice.

We thought we knew all about raising sons, but when Aaron arrived thirteen years after Mike, I had to re-educate myself. Aaron
had a highly-developed sense of independence. He felt he could do
everything on his own when he was three years old. He seemed hard-
er to control each day. He didn't take well to discipline.

One day Jan and I decided to begin a hug campaign. As often as
we could remember to do it, we would grab Aaron, give him a big
hug, and tell him we loved him. He hated it for a while. But the
time came when he began hugging back. He relaxed more and became more affectionate. It's not at all unusual now to hear his footsteps in the house at night and listen to his soft call, "You forgot to
hug me good night."

You can write to them. I never could tell my dad everything he
meant to me face-to-face. Too many years of avoiding such topics
made it a difficult barrier to cross. But I could plot it out in a letter.

Now I write to my boys when they're away at school, away at
camp, away at Grandma's, or whenever I'm away while they're at
home. A letter from home is terrific. A letter from Dad is a treasure.

You can surprise them. Do something they'd never guess you'd do.

Lori ran up to me and beamed, "Guess what happened on my
birthday. My dad, who has never worn a suit and tie since the day he
got married, rented a tux and took me out to dinner at that fancy
new French restaurant. Just me and him. He said he wanted me to
have a good memory of my sixteenth birthday. Boy, I'll never forget
it."

I couldn't imagine Lori's dad in a tux. He wears jeans more often
than I do. But caring dads send flowers or show up at recitals and ball
games when the kids thought they were too busy. They stay up late
helping build visual aids for science projects. They've even been
known to stand on rooftops and shout, "I've got the greatest kids in
the whole wide world!"

13

Caring Dads Leave the Door Open, the Porch Light On

Liz is a smart gal. At thirty-five she's worked her way up to vice president in an impressive California marketing firm. She's single, self-sufficient, and proud of her independence. She's the kind who will take a night school class in auto mechanics in order to repair her Seville.

Liz is drawing up plans for a new house in the country. She loves to ride half-wild horses and climb mountains.

Last December, during a violent rainstorm, Liz lost control of her car on the interstate. The Seville spun around several times and crashed into a center barrier. She suffered no serious injuries, but it left her shaken.

Later she confided in me, "You know what I said to the officer when he came to check on me? I told him over and over, 'I want my Daddy—I want my Daddy—' "

We never outgrow our need for a dad. Unfortunately, not all fathers seem to understand that.

Craig left home to wander the streets of Los Angeles when he was only twelve. He'd been kicked out of junior high for throwing a typewriter out the second-floor window. He'd been kicked out of the house because he threatened his mother with a steak knife. On and off drugs from age ten, Craig was a hard case at eighteen. That's when I met him.

A concert at the church attracted him. Within a few weeks God performed one of His miracles: Craig came to Christ. His hair still hung halfway down his back, and his beard still grew ragged. He still didn't have a steady job or much discipline. But a change began inside. It was a real conversion, and we watched the evidence week after week.

Three months later he had trimmed his hair, shaved his beard, and was working full time. He gave up the drugs and tried to study and apply the Bible.

"I want to go talk to my dad," he announced one day. "I want him to see I'm different."

Craig marched up to the door and knocked. His dad opened it. "Hi, it's me, Craig. Listen, I've got some things—"

"Get off my porch," was the only thing his dad said as he slammed the door.

Toward the end of the summer, Craig came in to talk. "I've finally figured out how I can reach my folks. I'm going to join the army. My dad's always talked about the big war and how it made a man out of him. Well, I'm going to enlist."

He did, and it was rough. But Craig had strong motivation. All through boot camp Craig fought against lifelong habits of anger and rebellion. And he finally made it through.

During his first leave, he stopped by the office to show off his green uniform and short haircut. "I'm going back to see my dad," he announced, as though his entire life centered on that impending moment.

Once again he was on the doorstep. "Dad, it's me, Craig. I'm in the army now. Can I come in and—"

"If you aren't off this porch in ten seconds, I'm going to call the cops!" were the last words Craig heard from his father.

That began another bout with drugs. A couple of AWOL's led to a discharge. Then there was a year of lost jobs and deep depression. But Craig survived. He's better now. He'll make it. Just don't try to tell him that God's like a loving father. He can't relate to that.

I wish Craig's case was an isolated event. But it isn't. We all need a refresher course in how important forgiveness is in a family. Jesus knew that. That's why He gives us such a clear description of it in the parable of the prodigal son in Luke 15.

The father in the story spotted his wayward son while he was still far down the road. Why did he see him so quickly? Because the old man probably spent lots of time staring down that road, just hoping for the day he'd return. The father "felt compassion for him, and ran and embraced him, and kissed him" (verse 20).

The father, not the son, did the running, embracing, and kissing. The son could barely tumble out his confession before the dad commanded that new clothes and jewelry be brought out and a feast prepared. It was time to celebrate—his son was home!

It's a powerful story of family forgiveness and provides some concrete guidelines for restoring family relationships.

Allow them to go. At some point we must allow our children to go their own way. We might not have bundles of money to shove in their hands, as the prodigal's father did. But just as we took the training wheels off their first bikes and nervously watched them wobble down the street, so we let them out the front door to wobble their way through life.

Keep an eye out for them. A call, a letter, a visit, an invitation to come by—make sure they know that their presence can make your day. Avoid the nags, guilt trips, and obvious attempts at interference into their lives, but make some sincere attempts to show them that you love them.

Forgive them if necessary. You don't have to be dishonest if you don't agree with their life-styles. But in a world where relationships are based on performance and friends remain true only as long as certain roles are played, let them know that home is a place they can return to and be themselves and find acceptance.

Forgiveness means you'll never bring up past offenses. It means you'll not blab to others what they may have done. It means you'll not sit around rehashing what they may have done to you.

Tell others you love them. The father in the parable threw a party. He knew people were more important than possessions. The son's inheritance was gone; it would never come back. But a son had returned. The father knew that in the end, sacks of money piled around a deathbed can bring little comfort. But loving children—sons, daughters, grandchildren—they are the true wealth of a man.

No one within shouting distance of that family farm had any doubt about the father's love for his wayward son.

But, someone is sure to say, that's all fine and good if your child chooses to repent and return home. But what if they don't want to come back? And, even tougher, what if they want to come back but refuse to change their offensive ways?

Good questions. Caring dads have the right to establish rules of the house that all members are expected to follow. You may love them and still not allow certain things to happen under your roof. Here are some ways to make family rules effective.

First, establish rules early. Let the little ones know the dos and don'ts. Teach them when they're young what they can expect as they grow older.

Second, follow biblical standards. Caring dads know and understand what the Bible has to say about family conduct. A dad who winks at an unmarried daughter's sleeping with her boyfriend is just as out of kilter as the dad who insists that no one of a particular racial group is allowed to enter his home. We must know the spirit and intent of the Bible's ethics and principles.

Third, allow room for discussion. Dads must be prepared to state why certain behavior is or is not accepted. Caring dads are open to consider alternatives.

Fourth, apply rules uniformly. Dads can't remove themselves from the jurisdiction of their own rules. If there's a rule against eating potato chips in bed, then it applies to everyone. If there's a rule about telling the others where you're going and when you'll be home, then dads comply too.

Fifth, family rules should be few. All of society works to keep us confined in boxes: "Walk," "Don't Walk," "Don't Walk on the Grass," "No Trespassing," "Pay by the fifteenth," "Use before February," and so on. There must be some place where we don't need a computer to remember all that's required of us. Make your rules clear, simple, and few in number.

Sixth, breaking rules isn't unforgivable. You take family rules seriously, but breaking them is not a capital offense. Jesus taught that we forgive seventy times seven for the same wrongs against us (Matthew 18:22; Luke 17:4). Look for repentance in the offender, a confession, and then practice forgiving from the heart.

Seventh, adult children establish their own rules. If they choose different rules from yours in their own homes, that's their right.

How can you be a good dad after they leave home? What are the guidelines for a continuing relationship?

First, work at being a good listener. When they stop by for a visit, turn off the TV, put down the newspaper, quit mowing the lawn, and hear what's on their minds. Their world's crammed with people who only listen to gain some kind of personal advantage. They need someone who's not trying to use them but just enjoys their presence. Ask a question or two in order to keep them talking.

My son Russell and I always talk about sports: baseball, football, basketball, street hockey, golf, tennis, marathons—you name it. I hadn't seen him in several weeks, so we had a lot of statistics to catch up on.

Fifteen minutes later, he led up to what he really came to talk about. He'd been thinking about quitting his job and going back to school. If I hadn't taken the time to listen, or had tried to dominate the conversation with my own interests, we'd never have gotten around to that life-changing discussion.

A caring dad is a stand-by advisor and assistant. At age twenty-two my married son's going to make a lot of decisions on his own. But if he wants my advice, he knows he can ask for it. He may go through a lot of situations in which I feel I've got plenty of advice to give. But if he doesn't ask me for it, I'll hold it in.

I'm also happy to assist with projects any time he requests my help. But they're his projects, not mine. I'll help him install his washer and dryer, replace a water pump, or refinish the furniture, but he's in charge. There's a difference between a willing hand and a dominating hand.

Second, be an avid fan. It starts when the little guy stumbles up to a T-ball stand and sends a slow dribbler that rolls beneath the first baseman's mitt and into right field. But somewhere between high school and marriage, we may think we've done our duty. We no longer root them on. We take down the pennants, put away the megaphone, and retire to the living room chair.

Kids of all ages need someone on their side. If that someone is their own dad, then the whole world stays in focus.

I'm just finishing my thirteenth book. Obviously I enjoy writing. My dad never had a chance to read one word in any of them; he died before I had anything in print. That's a great loss for me. I'd love to see the expression on his face when he looked at a shelf full of my titles, and I'd say, "Hey, Dad, did you ever think your kid would learn to do this?"

Third, even with adult children, continue to be a daddy. You added much to their lives when they were tiny. When they got scared, it was your hand they clutched. When they couldn't see the parade, it was your shoulders they sat on. When they wanted an ice cream cone, it was your pocket they tugged. When they scratched their knee, it was your lap they cried in.

When they built a house of blocks, they sought out your approval. When the neighbor kids didn't treat them right, it was your hug they wanted. When they struck out at the baseball game, it was your eyes they tried to avoid. When they learned the new trick on the bike, it was you they wanted to impress.

When they received honors at school, you were the first to see the trophy. When they met the perfect girl or guy, you were the important one to get introduced. When they got the promotion at work, you were the first person they called.

The reason's simple. You're their daddy—you always have been and always will be.

Daddy is the one who finds the way to tell his children, no matter what they do, no matter where they go, no matter how long it's been, no matter how old they are, no matter what it costs—

> If I have a penny, you'll never be broke.
> If I have a pork chop, you won't go hungry.
> If I have a shirt, you won't be cold.
> If I have an arm, you'll always be hugged.

And if I don't have a penny, or a pork chop, or a shirt, or enough power in my tired arms to hug anymore, come stand by my bed and hold my hand, and know that if there's a heart left in this old body, then Daddy still loves you.

14

Caring Dads Hug Moms

Parts of this book seem to insinuate that Dad has all the influence in the raising of children. Of course that's not true.

For instance, there are plenty of single-parent families today. Most of the ideas and examples in this book could be applied to them as well.

But this chapter takes a necessary turn. It was not God's original design for single parents to raise children alone. His plan called for a mom and a dad. For a variety of reasons, that ideal isn't always possible. And there are plenty of single parents doing a remarkable job of parenting. But here we will talk about a dad's relationship to his wife.

Caring dads show a life-long commitment to their wives through continual expressions of love and faithfulness. The Bible says, "For this cause a man shall leave his father and his mother, and shall cleave to his wife; and they shall become one flesh" (Genesis 2:24).

To "cleave" means to hold on tightly. It means to hug and hug and hug, and hug some more.

Some of the scenery on this earth makes me feel good to just be alive. I love the vast Western wilderness: the miles of open country, the high plateaus of Nevada, the big blue skies of the Montana plains, the rolling barren deserts of Arizona, the wheat fields of northern Idaho, the massive Sierras of California.

But sometimes the sight of people in certain situations does the same thing to me: the three-year-old playing with a bunny in his backyard, two junior high girls trying to catch the attention of the cute boy across the lobby at the airport, the young couple holding hands and looking at the jewelry store window in the shopping mall.

One of my favorite sights is to see the tender affection some elderly couples show each other in public. He struggles to lift himself out of the restaurant chair. With arthritic knees and stooped shoulders, he shuffles around to the other side of the table to hold the chair for his silver-headed queen. She rises slowly, smiles, and grips his arm. It's a weak and shaky arm, but she doesn't notice. She's held that arm a long time.

That's the same arm that helped her up into the Model T. It was that same arm that she clutched with nervous anticipation in her long white dress as they waited before the church altar to say, "I do." It was that arm that cradled her and told her he'd come back as soon as the war was over.

That arm held the babies. That arm never once failed her. It was right there, strong as ever, in the joys and the sorrows. She'd never have made it without him.

Those strong arms brought home the pay, built the house, mowed the grass, and put up the Christmas trees. That same arm led their daughter down the aisle and once again cradled babies. That is the arm that helped with dishes, rubbed a sore back, and brought comfort from nightmarish dreams. It's an arm she could count on.

I hear him say, "Come on, Princess, time to go home," as they toddle away.

Those are the scenarios of life that make me glad to be a part of God's human creation. The trouble is, there just aren't enough of those scenes around. On a recent radio interview I was asked what I thought was the number one problem in American family life. I didn't hesitate with my answer: "Lack of lifetime commitments." It's become too fashionable, too easy, to make all relationships disposable.

Tucked away in the book of Ecclesiastes is a terrific verse: "Enjoy life with the woman whom you love all the days of your fleeting life which He has given to you under the sun; for this is your reward in

life, and in your toil in which you have labored under the sun" (9:9).
The reward for our hard work is to be a lifelong love relationship
with our wife. That's what quality family life is all about. That's one
of the highest blessings given to us during our short stay on earth.
A lifetime commitment teaches many lessons.

First, you prove that God's plan does work. A man and woman together for life was God's idea. Too many folks criticize the plan before they've completed it. "It might be all right for others," they blurt
out, "but I can't live with such limitations." Too bad—they'll miss
the best part of life.

Second, you learn that a personal choice can solve most relationship problems. A long marriage works because two people choose to
make it work. That's how any healthy relationship is held together—
by a decision. Handling the pressures, tensions, and intimacy of marriage helps prepare you to overcome any obstacle in life.

Third, you learn that no one person is complete in himself. It takes
male and female to reflect God's image completely (Genesis 1:27).
We need other people to bring out God's best in us, and that must
evolve over a period of time.

Fourth, a lifetime commitment removes you from the competitive
game. You can set aside that inner drive that causes stomachaches in
teenage girls and fist fights among teenage boys. There's no more
need to impress the opposite sex with something you aren't. You can
get on with learning to enjoy being you. It's a good time of life.

Fifth, a lifetime commitment means you get to know one person
really well. And while you're getting to know your wife, she'll help
you to know yourself in a way that's impossible without her. Building
that kind of relationship is not easy, but it will propel you far ahead
of most of your contemporaries.

We're in marriage for the duration. There is no exit. No turning
back. No giving up.

But how can you keep on showing her how crazy you are about her year after year? The Bible has all kinds of suggestions. Here are a few.

Sacrifice something for her.
"Husbands, love your wives, just as Christ also loved the church and gave Himself up for her" (Ephesians 5:25).

Sacrifice: the giving up of something highly valued for the sake of someone else.

What's of great value to you? Here are some ideas to kick around.

- Turn off the Monday night football game. Tell her you want to spend the evening just with her.
- Put in some extra hours on the job all week so you can take off Friday at noon for a big weekend together.
- Drop out of the golf tournament. Use the entry fee to buy plants, and spend the weekend landscaping the flower bed, just the way she always wanted it.
- Sell the boat, and buy her that diamond ring she never got.
- Skip lunch, and buy her a rose every day this week.

If it doesn't hurt in some way, it's probably not a true sacrifice. But, in the last analysis, if you make sacrifices you will gain something even more precious.

Pamper her.
"So husbands ought also to love their own wives as their own bodies" (Ephesians 5:28).

It may be a little lumpy here and there, but you love it—your body, that is. We all love ourselves. Left to our own private devices, we know how to pamper ourselves. That's exactly how we need to treat our wives.

"To pamper" means to honor, even to the point of spoiling a little.

I try to spoil my wife. I want her to think that there's no guy on earth who would treat her this good. What are some ways to spoil a wife?

- Ask her to list three of her most dreaded jobs to do around the house, then do a couple of them.

- Make sure she has enough money in her wallet to buy something crazy once in a while. Don't make her accountable for the funds.
- Take her to dinner at the best place in town some time when its not a birthday or anniversary.
- Take her to a beauty salon and tell her to get the works: hairdo, manicure, pedicure, facial, and so on.
- Let her sleep in while you get the kids off to school.

Be a family spiritual leader.

"Bring them up in the discipline and instruction of the Lord" (Ephesians 6:4).

No family learns spiritual truth faster than the one who has a father who teaches and practices it.

You be the one who insists the whole family attend Sunday school as well as church.

You be the one who reviews the kids' memory verses and other take-home assignments.

Study up on the crucial theology issues of the times, and translate these into terms your whole family can understand.

You be the one that encourages spiritual commitment at each life change.

You be the one who suggests the family pray before meals, at the start of long journeys, and when your family makes important decisions.

Clean out the bitterness daily.

"Husbands, love your wives, and do not be embittered against them" (Colossians 3:19).

Bitterness is a parasite that adds nothing to life. It only sucks the vitality out of a relationship.

Remember that her failure to be perfect all the time is more than compensated for by the positive qualities that shine through most of the time.

Allow her mistakes to build something positive in her life and yours.

Remember, to say that you don't deserve the treatment you may receive one day is to imply you do deserve the good treatment of better days.

Grant her honor, understanding.
"You husbands likewise, live with your wives in an understanding way, as with a weaker vessel, since she is a woman; and grant her honor as a fellow heir of the grace of life, so that your prayers may not be hindered" (1 Peter 3:7).

Try to understand your wife's thought process, why she says and does certain things. Encourage her in her God-given talents and gifts and in her spiritual growth. Respect the things that are important to her.

Send her to the seminar she's been wanting to attend. Attend a family living conference with her. Take time with her afterwards to talk over how your family can apply the new things you've learned.

Start a daily reading program with her in some devotional literature as well as the Scriptures.

Encourage her to stretch and try new things.

Take care of her sexual needs.
"The husband does not have authority over his own body, but the wife does" (1 Corinthians 7:4).

We men can be very proficient in caring for our own needs and neglecting the needs of our wives. How do you find out about such things? Some open conversation, initiated by you, would do wonders.

Ask your wife what would be the most sexually-fulfilling evening she could imagine. Then see that her dream comes true.

Admit to your wife that you don't know everything about the subject, but pledge yourself to learning how to be the best lover possible.

Respect her moody times without putting a guilt trip on her about your own needs.

Tell her often how much her physical love means to you.

Trust her.
"The heart of her husband trusts in her" (Proverbs 31:11).

Show her that you believe you can count on her to do the right thing, even when you're not around.

Trust her with the new car. Don't give her a high school lecture about being careful or threats about the paint job.

Give her time to herself. Send her to her sister's in Hawaii. Let her have a day in the city. Don't demand a minute by minute accounting.

Trust her with decisions: what to buy your mother for Christmas, what kind of carpet for the family room, which first-grade teacher is best for Junior.

Put her name on all the bank accounts. Let her carry the travelers checks, the credit card, and the gold coin.

Praise her in public.

"Her husband also, and he praises her, saying: 'Many daughters have done nobly, but you excel them all' " (Proverbs 31:28-29).

If a friend only heard what you said about her in public, and only saw how you treated her then, what would he conclude about your relationship?

Never put your wife down as the core of a joke or jest.

Never comment negatively in public about her clothes or shape or looks.

Never interrupt her in order to improve her grammar or her way of expressing herself.

Never question her intellect or wisdom in public.

Never desert her at a gathering. Keep checking to see how she is getting along.

Never call her by a derogatory nickname.

Long-term relationships take a lot of effort. But it's worth it. Just ask my friend Lewis. We visited him the day his wife died.

Lewis married Lela in 1920. A doctor had warned him not to marry her. "She's sick, real sick. I don't think she'll last much more than a year."

"Well, I told him I'd marry her anyway. And she did have some sick years in the beginning. In and out of bed for almost three years—but then I got her up to the sanitarium in Santa Barbara. They helped her a lot. She was on her feet most times after that. Except when she was pregnant—

"I had to take care of the babies off and on. Sometimes her mother relieved us. I'd run home during my noon hour and cook us something to eat, change the diapers, and give them all a big hug.

"She liked to travel. When the kids grew up, we went everywhere together. She always acted like she was living on borrowed time—wanted to enjoy as much as she could. She lived to be eighty-three—not bad for a sick girl.

"Course, the past ten years or so, the illness caught up with her. Kept her in bed—"

Tears filled his eyes as he told me about those last years. "Finally, it affected her brain. She'd forget things—go for weeks not remembering who I was. But I kept her at home. It'll seem funny not having that routine anymore.

"I'd get up at four in the morning and rub her back. One hundred and seventy four rubs a day—I counted them; it was sort of my exercise too. Then I'd fix her breakfast. She loved poached eggs. The last year or so I had to feed her myself. Then I'd get her dressed, and if the weather permitted I'd take her for a walk around the backyard. She loved the outdoors. Two walks a day we took—

"On good days we'd make it all the way down the driveway to the front gate. Then, after lunch, I'd load her up in the car for a ride. She wasn't aware of too much, but I talked to her about the town, and the people, who was moving where, and what things used to be like.

"I can't get used to her being gone. Sixty-five years is a long, long time. It'll hit me hard tomorrow when there's no back to rub. But, boy, the old doc sure was wrong, wasn't he? She outlived him by fifty years.

"Guess I miss the hugging most. We were a huggy pair—guess I'll shed plenty of tears, but I guess sixty-five years of hugs ought to be enough for any man. Certainly a lot more than I deserved."

Caring dads keep right on hugging to the very end.

That's you and me.

We really do care.

If there was a flat fee we could pay to guarantee a happy, satisfied family, we'd figure out a way to raise the sum.

If there was a magical formula we could say to bring peace and love flooding into our homes, we'd shout it out.

If there was a space-age computer that could solve every family quarrel, we'd install one in every room.

We really care.

But the solutions to the struggles we face don't come easy. They require effort. Many times that means plugging away long after we'd rather give up.

Family success takes hard work. Sacrifice. Humility. Wisdom. Risk.

But you and I know it's worth it.

That's what makes us caring dads.

Moody Press, a ministry of the Moody Bible Institute, is designed for education, evangelization, and edification. If we may assist you in knowing more about Christ and the Christian life, please write us without obligation: Moody Press, c/o MLM, Chicago, Illinois 60610.